PENS UNDER THE SWASTIKA

A Study in Recent German Writing

W. W. SCHÜTZ

KENNIKAT PRESS
Port Washington, N. Y./London

PENS UNDER THE SWASTIKA

First published in 1946
Reissued in 1971 by Kennikat Press
Library of Congress Catalog Card No: 70-118415
ISBN 0-8046-1192-0

Manufactured by Taylor Publishing Company   Dallas, Texas

CONTENTS

PREFACE

THE longer the nightmare of Hitlerism and total war lasted, the more it seemed possible that the spirit of free men might be buried and crushed. Yet the more this danger increased, the clearer it became that it could not be. It was, therefore, like a revelation to come across the literature which had grown up inside Germany under the shadow of the Swastika, to find that pens had testified to eternal values and ideas at the very moment when Hitler seemed to be triumphant.

Both the unfailing belief and the discovery of this " hidden " literature would have been impossible without the friendship, assistance, and continuous support of a small circle of friends to whom the author and this study owe very much. In particular I should like to mention the Bishop of Chichester, the Rev. R. R. Williams, J. Carton, and Dr. Julius Rieger. Eric Fenn's advice, and his thorough correction of the style of this essay, have been as important as his continuous encouragement. Dr. Barbara Schütz-Sevin has done much of the necessary research.

W. W. SCHÜTZ

Richmond, Surrey
November 1945

INTRODUCTION

Is it right at all to speak of " another Germany "? What signs are there of its existence under the tide of Nazi terror, which is all the world has been able to see since 1933? To answer that question we have to do an almost impossible thing—impossible for those who have lived in a democracy and have not known what life was like under Nazi domination. We have to try to make ourselves realize the nature and the range of the Nazi Terror *from the inside*. Hitler's alternative for anyone who was unwilling to comply with the demands of the Third Reich has been made plain to us in the horrors of Buchenwald, Belsen and Dachau. But it is still difficult to realize what life must have been like with such threats for ever hanging over it. The Third Reich has been the classic example of totalitarian terror, unlimited by any restraint, physical or moral. Life under these conditions has been full of fear and silence for all who were not themselves the torturers and profiteers of this régime. Total war—millions of dead—hundreds of cities, towns and villages destroyed—all this has combined with the organized terror of the Gestapo and the S.S. to drive the citizen into a state of apathy and lethargy, which the invading armies of the Allies found everywhere. And, indeed, the whole machinery of the Third Reich seems to have been built with the deliberate purpose of creating this lack of will and initiative. They called it a " Führerstaat ". Leave everything to the Führer and his men—they will act, think and decide for all. This leadership bogy was the counterpart to the paralysis of the community. The people must follow blindly; and they could do so, for was there not

9

a leader who knew and did everything? All initiative which came from anybody but the leader was branded and persecuted as revolutionary.

For millions this kind of life seemed hard, often intolerable. But they were conscious, all too conscious, of their inability to do anything against it without proper leadership, organization and power. All this was missing. So many bowed both body and mind in order to escape the terror. But are we not entitled to ask whether there have been exceptions? This question may be important even for those who know Hitler only from hearsay. Is there anything in man which cannot be bent or broken by the terror of the totalitarian state? If there is, then there is a twofold hope. First, there may be, in very truth, a world of the spirit, which cannot be subdued by the world of terror and power; and, if that is so, then there is the further possibility that the world of power can be conquered from the bastion of the unconquerable spirit. However powerful and unassailable the power-state, the totalitarian system, may appear at certain moments of its victorious evolution, there remains always the hope, perhaps the certainty, that it may yet be assailed and conquered from that seemingly unreal corner where there is nothing but the spirit, nothing but the idea of freedom, of the eternal soul of man.

The question whether there is such a bastion of the unconquerable spirit has often been asked during the centuries. But rarely has there been a situation in which man lost all physical and material power to oppose, indeed to fight, the oppressor. Rarely, therefore, has it been possible to separate spiritual and moral resistance almost entirely from its backing and environment of power. For the most part, there was in the past some powerful individual, or group, or state, or at least some powerful knowledge, which made physical revenge possible against all tyrants and gave strength to open spiritual and moral witness.

It was in most instances possible to find a safe corner even in a seemingly all-powerful state. The pure word of art, whatever motives might lie behind it, was sheltered by a " safety-belt ", which still existed, even in such nearly totalitarian circumstances.

The efforts of the Third Reich to surpass all previous attempts at totality and terror were succeeding very well before they were checked on the battlefields of Europe. World opinion regarded the victorious aggressions of 1938-39 as the last attempt of Nazism to assert itself. In consequence, the claim of the victorious tyrants to have absorbed or, indeed, quelled all ideas and thinkers who might have opposed their victorious rule, found an all too ready credence. These years of Nazi triumphs constituted the climax of state power. Any deviation from the victorious path of the conquerors appeared, to most of those who lived under their rule and were cut off from the outside world, altogether pointless and useless. There was no power in sight—whether inside Germany or outside—which could match the power of Hitler. There was no organization left which commanded sufficient force and cohesion to challenge the Third Reich.

Consequently the stage was set, as rarely in history, for the expression of principles and ideas based almost entirely on spiritual foundations without much hope of external support. There was no organization, there were no weapons, and, alas, for most of those men and women, there was no hope of escape. The surrounding world had practically closed its doors, and had decided against anything like an adequate support for those who dared to stand up against the régime.

Consequently, we find almost all the power arrayed on the side of the Third Reich, and practically no physical force available to its opponents. To them spiritual, moral, intellectual power was all they could muster. The antagonism between power and spirit was almost complete. The time had come for the spirit to prove its indestructible character.

This experience has a significance which goes far beyond the frontiers of any single country. It is a test-case. However modest and however narrow in range the expression of spiritual values and moral principles, of artistic beauty and scientific objectivity may have been in Nazi Germany, every sign of it must be acknowledged as a deed of freedom against the totalitarian claim of total subjugation. In the history of a nation the great achievements of even a few great men may lend colour and splendour to the name of that country. In the case of the Third Reich only later generations will be able to estimate correctly the comparative importance of whatever active or passive resistance, attempted revolts or oppositional organizations may come to light now that Hitler has fallen. It is not the purpose of this book to go into that. Neither is it suggested that what may be unearthed should be considered as of significance in forming a true political judgment about Germany. The material available is still quite insufficient for that. It is still impossible to draw up a balance-sheet of responsibilities for the many crimes which have been committed in Europe since 1933.

While, however, there is no basis for a political book, something quite different is possible. It is possible to point to the existence of men and books, preachers and sermons, writers and writings, historians and histories, teachers and teachings, where the flame of freedom was never extinguished. This is more than most people expected. With that lack of moral and intellectual integrity which has become such a tragic after-effect of totalitarian propaganda, many have accepted the assertion of Hitler that there was nothing inside Germany but the Nazi creed. This, at any rate, has proved wrong. There are traces, more than that, there is evidence to the contrary. In order to find it one has to approach this field in exactly the same manner and with the same methods which any historian would use to explore a distant and unknown period of history.

This method is necessary because the ways and means of life in a totalitarian country are so utterly different from those in a liberal democracy. There is only one possible way to speak openly and frankly on political matters, and that is within the framework of the dictatorial machine and ideology. If one expresses thoughts which are in line with the Party, then, indeed, there is no *fortissimo* which may not be used. If, however, anything outside this fearful realm of oppression is said or written, then a completely different method of expressing thoughts is necessary.

Carefully chosen quotations, symbolic narratives, significant omissions, these and innumerable other means are used in order to convey genuine and free thought. The historian, or the simple reader who approaches this kind of literature with eyes which can only read obvious and blatant things, will find but little of significance. But this is a wrong impression, because this superficial reading does not get at the real meaning of such writings.

In order to understand what these authors who have published " free " literature under Nazi dictatorship really mean, it is necessary to try to see with the eyes and to listen with the heart of somebody who has had to live in their circumstances. This is what an historian would have to do if he wanted to write a history of ancient Rome, or of any period where he must rely on nothing but faint memories, documents, and seemingly unconnected bits and pieces of evidence. This is what we must do if we want to understand the meaning and importance of those documents which have reached the outside world from the Third Reich.

The reasons which make it necessary for the historian to think in terms of somebody who was living at the period he is dealing with are doubly valid in case of a totalitarian régime. In addition to the estranging factors of time and space there is the paramount fact of force. All signs of life are petrified by the existence of the terror. Individual utterances become infinitely more scarce and precarious than in any other form of state and society. There may be an infinite variety of personal emotions, thoughts, aspirations, for all we know. But whatever there is of good or bad will lie below the surface. For, in principle, there is only one voice—the voice of the régime. There is only one opinion, one aim, one faith, one—leader. It is an artificial, terrorized oneness which confronts us, whether we trust it and believe in it or not.

This impression of artificial unity has to be reckoned with by the historian. How much more has it to be reckoned with by somebody who has to live in such a state! For the historian it is a matter of understanding, knowledge, interpretation. For those who live there it is a matter of life and death.

Again, there are many contradictory things with which anybody who wants to understand things over there has to reckon. One is that this unity is hardly ever fully achieved. There are always remnants of older beliefs, tendencies towards this or that development, inherent in the gigantic state machine. More than that, while there is always this life and death question connected with even the slightest deviation from the official path, it often does not arise in practice. One cannot be sure, one can never be sure, when freedom is

lost—when the extreme case, the case of total destruction,
the case of death, really does occur. In the Third Reich it
has occurred to many at the most unexpected places and at
odd times. Not all Socialists, Communists or Liberals lost
their lives in 1933. Some were killed in 1933. Some were
murdered in 1934. Some were assassinated in 1938. Others
were murdered inside concentration camps in 1944. But
some were released from concentration camps after years of
imprisonment during the War. In other words, it is not a
case of do or die. One never knows how, where, when
one may have to die—or do.

This may seem strange to our historian who tries to think
himself into the experience of a totalitarian country. But,
on second thoughts, he may change his view. If, as has
happened under tyrants, everybody who is known to be an
antagonist of the régime is either killed or exiled, the
country may settle down after the first wave of terror has
passed over it. People may begin to breathe more freely
again. They may believe that those who have not been
destroyed by the first impact of dictatorial fury may now
venture to live. It is wrong to say that under all dictator-
ships there is never room for human greatness. Hardly any
period has achieved such an accumulation of talent as
the Renaissance under the city-tyrants of Italy. French
literature flourished under Louis XIV.

Consequently our historian will have to look closer at
the peculiar system of totalitarianism which developed inside Germany after 1933. He will find that the *threat* of
death and torture did more to establish a rule of terror
than death and torture themselves. The Gestapo saw to
it that it never remained an empty threat. Yet this system
of totalitarianism, under whose deadly shadow Europe had
to live for twelve years, never penetrated the last corners
of national or private existence. Fortunately it did not have

time. It relied on the paralysing effects of the threat of terror just as much as on terror itself for the establishment of its unchallenged rule.

Here, then, appears one of the discrepancies in the totalitarian system. On the one hand, the demand for the complete surrender of all personal opinions and freedom of expression; and yet, on the other, spheres of thought and self-expression which the Nazi never penetrated. Our historian will be torn between the notion, unsimplified by propaganda, of a totalitarian system which allows of no free scope, and the far more complicated reality of a terror applying itself in decrees, and with a variety of methods and purposes. Here the Fascist state thought it hardly worth while to strike, for it saw nothing but " artistic play " and " intellectual forlornness ". There the same state felt alarm and struck—for instance, if it was faced by priests and Churches.

How easy for our historian to conclude that in these circumstances opposition must have been easier than it was made out. And yet, let him use his imagination and ask himself how far he himself would have risked not only his own existence, but the existence of wife and children, for, say, the distribution of a political leaflet. After all, there are people who do that, although it is obvious that in some nations there are too few of them.

Our historian, then, may land where all great historians have landed—where things political and things human meet. He may begin to build that bridge which connects historical events with the reader and, indeed, the writer of history, namely, the bridge of human experience and political clarity. He may see that there have been, and there are, chances of freedom even in a totalitarian régime, if and when a few unbreakable spirits dare to take them. He will realize how rare this greatness has been, and is likely to be, in history; but he will take heart that it has never failed altogether.

But obviously this is not all. This is an approach and a method; there is nothing hard and fast yet to go on. If there be such instances of unbreakable spirit and of courage for the sake of freedom, of humanity, of love, of God—how can they be found? Realizing the dangerous circumstances in which these manifestations had to be created, we shall hardly look round in the market-place for their advertisement. Certainly we shall not be likely to find them in the Nazi papers or Goebbels' radio. The very conditions of danger and terror under which these men and women had to live make it plain that special methods would be needed to give these works and ideas as wide a circulation as possible, without making it too easy for the Gestapo to step in and finish it all at a stroke.

There have been underground-presses and leaflets and slogans painted on walls during the dark nights of black-out and war. There have been organizations and political doings and schemes. There have been escapes and assistance to those who wanted to escape—prisoners of war, slave-labourers, Jews, men of the 20th July, and others. There has been unceasing whisper-propaganda against the régime and the War, ridicule of the leaders, and the unearthing of internal corruption. There have been thousands of refugees and exiles who joined the fighting forces of the Allies against the Third Reich in the West and in the East. There has been assistance for Resistance movements, and there have been tens of thousands of dead on the Home Front—killed by the Gestapo. All this there has been, and obviously it has not been enough. But what there has been will have to be assessed later, when all the material will be available, and the political account can be settled.

This is, therefore, not where the historian will have to

look if he wants to find his evidence. What matters is not so much the camouflaged youth group, or the harmless air-raid warden who chalks slogans on the walls. What matters here is less the unpolitical soldier who lets a member of the Resistance pass across the frontier into Switzerland, nor yet the man with a new name who fights in the F.F.I. It is not even the leaflet which he may be presented with; for that might just as well have come from a printing-press in London and found its way into Germany via the R.A.F., as from the secret printing-press in Cologne, which no longer exists.

Where, then, can one look? There have been only two major fields of activity' where, even during the height of Nazi power in the course of the War, others than the Nazis and their hirelings could keep in touch and express themselves freely, or rather as freely as circumstances, caution and camouflage permitted: books and the Churches. Obviously, there were still the factories where workers met. There were the fields where peasants met. There were the excursions where youths met. Whatever opposition to the régime arose amongst these groups can be traced somehow to these meeting-places. But, again, this would lead us on to a region which cannot be measured and recognized yet. But there is no doubt of the very clear evidence afforded by books and pulpits.

There is more to it than mere political significance. What we are concerned to know is whether and how far the human spirit can prevail against the impact of power. There is, therefore, a deeper meaning in this discovery that books and the writers of books and sermons have maintained the integrity of their faith, the essence of truth, the calling of human love, against the demands and threats of totalitarian terror.

I. CAMOUFLAGED LITERATURE AND THE INTEGRITY OF WRITING

BOOKS, and often also sermons, bear the mark of the circumstances in which they have been written. Only very rarely does an author dare to call a spade a spade. This frankness—heartening though it is under certain circumstances—has its dangers in a totalitarian land, not only for the author, but also for the book. For an unguarded word, a rash challenge, and the book might never reach a single reader. The Gestapo might intervene.

Just because this literature of freedom had a purpose beyond the mere self-fulfilment of a free mind, it had to be given such a form that the publisher could bring it before the public. This purpose of reaching the reader must have remained paramount. It is easy to see in many instances that the writer or the preacher could hardly have had any illusions about the potential danger in which he stood the moment his words left his study. Yes, there was camouflage, and the historian will have no difficulty in separating camouflage from essence and meaning. But for the writer or the preacher this camouflage must always have appeared too thin, too vague to protect him against the revenge of the state. For what good would a camouflage be which was so heavy and so thick that not even the most sympathetic reader could see through it? A balance had to be struck between the necessity of playing for safety until the words reached the proper audience, and the necessity of saying things clearly enough to be understood by that audience. Different authors struck different balances: but some balance had always to be struck.

This does not mean that all literature which is important

for keeping up the spirit of independence, faith, or reason comes into this category at all. The Bible has become powerful in social life once more. The demand for Bibles in Germany went up steadily. The Old Testament, and to a certain extent the New Testament, became central to a struggle which Christians could not give up.

The Classics

The study of the classics has become an important factor in the evolution of spiritual resistance. New series of classical works have been published under the Nazi régime and in the course of the War in particular. These enterprises were deliberate and not merely chance publications. Their aim was to keep the great classical tradition alive against the growing impact of the destructive Nazi ideology. It is easily forgotten that this ideology decried the traditions of humanism, of Greek and Roman civilization, of philosophy and reason. It is easily assumed that it was easy to maintain this tradition against the threatening displeasure of a totalitarian régime. That may be, but it has to be done by somebody, if the tradition is not to die. It has been done.

There is, for instance, the Sammlung Dieterich in Leipzig which has published standard works, like *The Tragedies and Fragments of Æschylus,* Hesiod's works, Pindar's *Poems and Fragments,* a selection of works of Seneca, and others. It would be dull to give the full list of over one hundred works which have appeared in spite of Rosenberg and Goebbels. Great French writers, like La Rochefoucauld, Montesquieu, Ligne, Balzac; great English literature, like Bacon's *Essays,* and a new edition of *Hamlet,* with notes by Professor Schücking, are amongst them.

Another series on similar lines is the Tusculum library,

bi-lingual editions of works by Æschylus, Euripides, Solon, Tibullus, and other ancient poets. These books are inexpensive, but printed on good paper and in good type. In this series the classics are printed in their original language— Greek or Latin—on the left-hand pages, the German translation on the right page. Schücking's *Hamlet* edition uses the same method for English and German.

A popular edition of classical works which had appeared long before the Nazis' rise to power, the Kröner edition, was also continued. Similarly the famous Reclam, Insel, Göschen editions were continued and provided the readers with much genuine reading material, with classical literature, objective text-books, philosophical works, foreign writings. Occasionally the publishers accepted Nazi-infected literature, obviously in many cases in order to be able to continue their main line of publication.

As far as these classical and standard works were concerned it is obvious that there was hardly any need of political camouflage. The relative importance of this continued effort to keep reason and judgment alive must be studied later. But anyone who has lived in a totalitarian country knows how invaluable it is to be able to buy such books and to read what has remained greatest in human thought and creation.

Yet if you know anything of the burning actuality of some of these classical authors, you will realize that while considerations of day-to-day policy did not enter into the making of these books, some of the outstanding ones contain what amounts to political dynamite. To put it at its simplest, there is a wealth of political wisdom in some of these ancient writings which cannot but exert an educative influence on a society which has been deprived of all political education by its rulers. There are also many profound observations about freedom and dictatorship, about the essence of democracy and the dangers of tyranny in some of these books which were fully appreciated and made people want to read them. A striking example of such border-line cases is the sudden and almost vehement interest in Jakob Burckhardt's *Letters.*

In such cases censorship provided a comparatively slight obstacle simply because the totalitarian masters were little concerned with writers who were long since dead. Any real appreciation of history, any true sense of historical values and realities has been singularly lacking in this movement which claimed to usher in a " thousand years' dominion " without knowing anything about the lessons of the previous thousand years! An exaggerated sense of power made those in control of the Third Reich look with scorn on the seemingly ridiculous efforts of some of their slaves to maintain this altogether pointless pastime called culture. What, indeed, could words do against guns?

If we look at the quantity of genuine free literature produced under the shadow of the swastika, we find, therefore, that reprints of old works, new editions of classical writings, and commentaries on art and history rank in the forefront. It is difficult to give any exact number of books sold during this war, but from the titles and the number of cheap editions one can guess that they run into millions. Yet these publications only cover the widest and in principle least political section of the audience. There has been a continuous flow of literature which we shall have to classify as history, but which owing to its semi-political nature appeared far less frequently than the original classical works.

Biographies

In an age which is so clearly dominated by popular, or

would-be popular, leaders, by impressive or terrible personalities, it is only natural that there should be interest in the great figures of political life—not, of course, contemporary German leaders, for they were always presented as incarnations of wisdom—but in figures in the past. So we find biography occupying an important place.

Altogether a considerable number of biographies have appeared, which were written, if not with the purpose of illuminating the contemporary scene, at any rate with an often unmistakable sense of the parallels between the past and the present. A recent example in English literature would be Arthur Bryant's books on the Napoleonic Wars, with their clear comparisons between, for instance, Napoleon and Hitler. This type of biography or monograph has had some importance in the evolution of free thought in the Third Reich. Needless to say, in the long run, the totalitarian system realized the significance of this type of writing and tried to make use of it for its own ends. Highly coloured and falsified biographies of Frederick the Great and Napoleon were written by official Nazi authors who painted Hitlerite features into the historical portraits. But somehow or other this attempt of the régime failed, presumably because its own characteristics were too real and ever present for any intellectual or spiritual, political or psychological interpretation to succeed.

One or two publishers—including Piper and Callwey—specialized in biographies and biographical novels which became popular and helped thousands of people to a new understanding of political personalities and processes. Two trends seem to have prevailed. One trend is towards the closer understanding of really great men, like Alexander the Great and Caesar. Joseph Gregor published a biography of Alexander the Great. Droysen's famous biography was re-edited by Professor Berve and published by Kröner in a cheap edition. Matthias Gelzer's *Julius Caesar* was published by Callwey in 1941. It was based on an earlier essay published twenty years previously, but strikingly more relevant now.

The other trend shows a remarkable interest in the history of men who stood at the beginning of the decline of their countries. Altogether, periods of decline, of disaster, and even of degeneration seem to have exacted some attraction. The decline of the Roman Empire was a major subject of study and observation. The reasons for this are not difficult to find. They are partly the hope of the oppressed intelligentsia that the tyrannical power of their state would be broken by some historical factor or another, even if the War should fail to bring liberation. Partly, they are based on the feeling that modern tyranny was merely the prelude to historical decline, even though clothed in seemingly splendid conquests and victories.

Ludwig Pfandl's Spanish trilogy dealt with the Spanish Empire at its height and its fall under the assault of France and England, with a particularly interesting detailed study of Philip IV and Charles II. The translation of Bidez' *Julian,* which was published in 1940, is another revealing example.

It was not that these biographies were nothing but concealed portraits of contemporary tyrants and conquerors, or of present-day suffering. These and similar books did not just use history as a cloak for political ideas. There have been such cases. Harden's *Caligula,* a pamphlet directed against Emperor William II, is an example. But most of these works were genuine works of art and historiography. It is part of their importance that they are genuine, that they are scientific and artistic works, that there is no falsification and no bending of the truth in them. For the truth, inherent in great writing, has its own inescapable value even in a highly politicized world, and particularly when the task is one of standing up against the distortions and tortures of a totalitarian state.

Yet somehow and somewhere the historian who reads these works, and tries to read them as if he had to read them in a lonely room behind drawn curtains, with the Gestapo watching outside, finds them highly topical. He knows that Thucydides or Seneca or Jakob Burckhardt could not possibly have meant what the author is trying to say, and that the real meaning lies hidden. Faces begin to look like masks. Behind the features of historical figures you begin to discern the outlines of contemporary character. Behind the developments of times long past you begin to recognize the trends of your own time. Historical judgments acquire the quality of political pronouncements.

History as Politics

There are, however, books which deliberately made use of the opportunities of historical camouflage—political writings under the guise of history. That is an old ruse which has been used by Roman, French and English writers. It was used during this war by German authors who wanted to attack the Nazi régime. It is often difficult to draw the line where history begins and politics end. Some of these books are sound historical writings, and yet they serve the political purpose. Frank Thiess' *Empire of the Demons* is an example. The circle of people reached by a book like this—calling itself a novel—must have been considerable. For it was published by Zsolnay in a first edition of ten thousand copies. It was voluminous—nearly seven hundred pages—and, in the existing scarcity of books, must have been handed from reader to reader and from family to family. Thiess would appear to be a liberal, but the novels of Bergengruen, which come under the heading of historical novels proper, show the marks of traditional Protestant conservatism.

Another type of camouflaged literature is the philosophical or sociological treatise, dealing with the ideas of great thinkers and yet containing a large number of topical observations by the author of the book. For instance, Alfred von Martin's essay on the Renaissance and analysis of *Burckhardt und Nietzsche* are masterpieces in their own way. Martin gives the key to his work on Burckhardt and Nietzsche in the preface to the book, which was published in 1941. He declares that he uses the biographical details merely as the starting-point in order to arrive at a systematic description of the " human and intellectual systems " which they represent. He wants to show " the important principles which reach far beyond the individual case ", " two worlds which oppose each other ". In this way he is able to deal with such problems as " Power ", " The End of Freedom? ", " Living Dangerously? ", " Individualism and Greatness ", " Ancient Régime and Revolution ", and finally " Europe and the Problem of Power and Freedom ". One can imagine what these chapter-headings would mean to those who had hardly heard anything like it for years.

The art of concealment found yet other expressions. It is natural that where the wide cloak of history ended, human imagination should find ever new forms of pictures and symbols, which, by their very novelty, proved useful disguises for a little while. Expressionism in art and literature were not altogether extinguished in spite of the hostility of the régime to everything which was not platitudinous. Perhaps it was part of the inferiority complex of the Nazi régime which prompted their violent antagonism to everything which was not plainly understandable to each and every one of them.

They feared hidden hostility behind what was to them the unknown. But the larger part of art and knowledge was unknown to them. Their fears and hatred proved not altogether unfounded, for there are examples of fantastic works of art which carried a political message and which concealed a violent attack against the foundations of the régime. Books by Ernst Jünger and Friedrich Georg Jünger, etchings by Weber and others, come into this category.

Now, our historian, looking at these camouflaged words, each of which had also a real life of its own, has to ask himself how anybody could penetrate the camouflage to the deeper meaning of these things. It is obvious that camouflage can be overdone, that the real meaning may be hidden so deeply that practically nobody will ever find it.

There is evidence by many who have been inside the frontiers of the " New Order " that this fear is without foundation. These books and these authors have become famous because of their courage. Their message has been understood. It appears that this process of understanding what must have been a surprising revelation to thousands was gradual. It also seems to have varied in degree. Some readers seem to have looked for nothing but the political element contained in these books. Others took them at their face value and began to wonder only gradually. Others enjoyed the art and saw the message. At any rate, there is no evidence that anything like an organized political movement was created by this literature. An " organization " cannot spring into existence merely by the force of the written word.

Educational Efforts

At the same time there is evidence that something resembling a public opinion was, indeed, fostered by such writ-

ings. Those who, like the American correspondents in
Berlin up to 1942, like neutral pastors or visitors, have
studied the situation closely—and by no means all of them
have—have come across the vestiges of these results. In
some cases a more clearly defined audience can be traced.
This is more easily recognizable in the case of text-books
and classical works than when we have to deal with novels,
poetry, art and the like. The latter create a mood, an outlook, even a tendency of thought; they may even create
habits and standards of behaviour, as, indeed, has happened
in Germany amongst a circle of men and women who have
acquired the outlook of the authors whom they value. This
is even true of readers of almost entirely unpolitical writers
who merely kept alive the tradition of language and writing
which the Nazi authors destroyed.

But the students of more profound works are bound to
be educated by their contents and aim. This has become
very apparent during the War when the universities again
and again produced groups of young people who showed a
political courage so sadly lacking amongst most other
citizens, comparable only to the old cadres of organized
Labour. There we find the traces of an educational process which tends to shape the whole of the man.

In this educational process which reached not only university students, but—as the Munich revolt and other
instances have shown—also secondary school boys and
girls, and even extended to the working classes, a number
of old university teachers combined with young ones. The
younger teachers have remained almost unknown outside
Germany. One or two were captured at the front and
are now in Allied prisoners-of-war camps. Others will become known slowly in the post-war period. Amongst the
older generation we find men like von Martin, Ritter,
Brandi, Spranger, Vossler, Meinecke, Andreas.

Not all of those who remained upright in matters of learning and science, who kept the flame of knowledge and reason and of the arts burning, have kept equally straight in daily politics. It is a strange experience that in these days of strain and stress many weakened in some respects, although proving brave and unbreakable in others. Some of those whom we have mentioned, and others who will appear in the later chapters of this book, compromised with the régime in matters of Party membership, war service, and similar things. In some cases it is quite obvious that this course was the only one which enabled the man to continue writing and publishing, teaching and lecturing. To use a military metaphor, they withdrew on one part of the front in order to hold another part. How far each individual was justified in this action may only become clear much later.

Of course, you could remain silent—and many a writer or scholar has done so. Some—but not all—had the chance of emigration. Some refused this, through fear of foreign languages and customs, preferring their private homes even at the cost of political defeat. There have been particularly unfortunate cases, such as that of Karl Jaspers, one of the greatest of living philosophers, and of tremendous import-' ance for contemporary thought. He was deprived of his chair at Heidelberg, but could not find any permanent employment at any university abroad. The great lawyers Anschütz and Radbruch are other examples. Though cut off from their academic activities inside Germany, the influence of their personalities cannot have remained altogether negligible, limited, very limited though it must have been.

But there have been more fortunate men, such as August Grisebach, who became Professor of Philosophy at Zürich. He has published two or three text-books in the course of the War which were published by Paul Haupt in Bern.

Haupt has also an office in Leipzig, and in this way Grisebach's books reached students inside Germany. These books were plainly intended as text-books, as teaching material for students who might not have a tutor or lecturer with them. They deal with profound questions of philosophy, sociology, and thought by putting questions which are answered in the following paragraphs. Thus, *The Question of the Fate of Europe* is subdivided into 130 questions, such as " The Present State of Truth ", " Why is the Crisis of the World combined with a Crisis of Religion? ", " Can Sociology contribute to Reconstruction? ", " Why is the critical faculty essential for Reconstruction? ", " What is the Ethos of Labour in the Europe of the Future? ".

There has also been literature published in Switzerland which did not reach Germany openly. The outstanding case is that of Karl Barth, the Protestant theologian, whose writings became essential for the Church Resistance, not only in Germany but throughout Europe. He has lived in Basel for the past ten years, and his books were published there, but much that has happened inside the Confessional Church —many a sermon, class, or lecture—could not have been carried out without the firm basis of Barthian theology. Some copies of his books have always reached Church opposition circles inside the Nazi frontiers. Others were read by students and visitors who came to Switzerland. There is, then, a definite place for Barth's writing in the Church-struggle, and some of his ideas were part and parcel of the ideological war which has been going on on the northern side of the Rhine, even though Barth himself was unable to cross the frontier which he could see from the windows of the university, where he had been teaching ever since 1934.

These, then, are some, at least, of the more important ways in which literature, teaching and preaching could be carried on even inside the dangerous realm of totalitarian tyranny. They are not, of course, complete, and more will certainly come to light.

The Importance of Style

But it would remain altogether too incomplete a picture if no mention was made of yet another vehicle which transmitted ideas in spite of the watchful eye of Nazism. This vehicle is the language, the peculiar style itself which has been developed. The typical Nazi author always tried to cover up his lack of ideas and his incoherence by a spate of words which sounded impressive and meant nothing. Hitler himself carried this habit a stage further, and as often as not, used words which meant something quite different from what he obviously wanted to convey. To put it bluntly, he just misused words altogether. The disciples of the Führer realized this, but acclaimed it as possessing an irrational forcefulness. In this way a typical Nazi style was developed, so grotesque and blatant that it is usually sufficient to read only a few lines in order to detect Nazi authorship.

In contrast with·this rapid and ugly decline the oppositional authors developed, each in his own way, a distinct style, which became no less significant than the Nazi jargon. Some, like the great novelist Wiechert, are subtle in the use of words and use a fine brush and soft colours. Some, like Ernst Jünger, have created a new synthesis between realism and symbolism. The pictures which Jünger, once a leading nationalist writer, uses in his *Marmorklippen* are altogether fantastic, but they are symbolical and can be deciphered by the careful reader, as deciphered they have been. At times almost brutal in his descriptions of reality, he is yet sparing

with words. This combination of few words, full of meaning, with fantastic scenery, has given to Jünger's writings
a strange and powerful attraction. *Marmorklippen* was perhaps the most influential book published during the past
few years: yet the censor could hardly object when no persons, towns or countries are referred to by name in its
pages. The events take place in a country which belongs
seemingly to the world of fairies. The men have strange
and unusual names. The furniture, the weapons, the entire
scenery belong to various centuries in a strange mixture of
ancient and modern. But in this fantastic world the great
tragedy of the opposition against the Third Reich is pictured—two brothers, trying to live their own life devoted
to science and nature, are gradually drawn into the turmoil
which reaches their " marble cliffs ". They have to fight
for their very lives and, in the end, they have to flee into
Switzerland. Timelessness is used both as an artistic
medium and as political camouflage.

The contrast between the unreality of the scenery and
names on the one hand and the brutal reality of the real story
on the other hand, is striking. This same experience is less
dramatic, but equally symptomatic in Jünger's diary of the
campaign in France. The same puritan language, the same
realism, the same scarcity of words, behind which we feel
so often the burning heart and the political appeal.

You find much the same kind of thing in the outstanding
utterances of Church leaders, Catholic and Protestant. They
possess a vigour which has been lacking in most utterances
of the Church for decades. At times they seem less like
religious formulas than expressions of an experience in
which divine power and earthly danger confront each other.
Some of Bishop Galen's or Archbishop Groeber's utterances
have all the prophetic extremism of the Old Testament. A
simple comparison between some of these sermons and dec-

larations and similar documents issued by ordinary churchmen in less dangerous times shows the change which has
taken place.

This new language hid some things and revealed others.
People began to read more carefully. Books became
precious, at any rate such books, such statements, at the
very moment when newspapers lost all respect because they
prostituted themselves to the régime. The new language
left a thousand things unsaid, which our historian, accus-
tomed to democratic usage, would expect to find expressed
fully and plainly. Political issues of the day—the War,
Strength through Joy, all the other items which filled the
columns of the newspapers—never appeared in any of these
writings. The names of the leaders were *taboo*. Nothing
which could be labelled political by any censorship appeared.
Instead, we find political principles discussed theoretically.
What would be a practical, to-the-point appeal in a democratic country becomes a theoretical treatise dealing with
the rights and wrongs of centralized government in a totalitarian state. The language loses colour and gains inner
meaning. It becomes less clear on the surface, and more
profound.

II. THE LONGING FOR FREEDOM

In the heart of the Third Reich, amid the long, dark shadows of terror, freedom could not be destroyed.

It is, of course, a comparatively easy task to point out that tens of thousands of freedom-loving men inhabited the concentration camps. In October 1943 Himmler revealed that then there were 40,000 political prisoners and 70,000 " a-social " elements in his camps. It is obvious enough that these tens of thousands, their families, their friends, their followers, longed for freedom, for liberation from their enslavement and suffering. Oppression always brings its own Nemesis: its enemies, who, ever anew, seek freedom. The harder the oppression, the deeper the longing for freedom among the oppressed. In the strange cycle of life, freedom can be born out of slavery, and, alas, slavery out of freedom.

But the history of the Third Reich has proved that there is more to it than that. It has shown that freedom for one group may leave another group in darkest slavery. We therefore hesitate to underline a series of individual pleas and actions for freedom which were plainly undertaken by people who had their own interest at heart, but cared comparatively little for freedom as such, for freedom for the nation and for mankind. Such interventions did take place —for instance, when certain industrialists attempted to ward off too much state interference.

The Voice of the Churches

The charge has been made against the Churches that they, too, have spoken only in order to safeguard their own position and prerogatives. Dr. Temple, the late Archbishop of Canterbury, who launched that attack, later declared that he had been misinformed and that, in reality, the Churches had stood up bravely against Nazism. What are the facts? In the course of the War there have been a number of speeches, sermons, Pastoral Letters from Catholic Bishops which dealt with the problem of the totalitarian state, and of freedom as opposed to this state. These documents show that they have had their origin in the defence by the Churches, of their own life: only later do they show a growing concern with individual freedom and the " natural rights " of man. The border-line is often only dimly recognizable. On July 13th, 1941, Count Galen, Bishop of Münster, spoke of "a frightful thing that happened among us yesterday ", referring to the confiscation of Church property. He went on to protest against the actions of the Gestapo in other parts of Europe and of Germany, in Western Poland, in South Germany, in the newly conquered territories, in the Vosges, Luxemburg, Lorraine. Here, again, he speaks of the treatment of Catholic priests, monks, nuns. But then he goes further and declares: " Before the physical superiority of the Gestapo forces, every German citizen is without protection and without defence . . . This is something that many German citizens have experienced for themselves in the course of the last year " (*German Home Front*, page 250). The first public indictment of the Gestapo!

In the Joint Pastoral Letter of the German Bishops published in 1943 we find a still stronger demand for the " rights of man which have their basis in God's rights ". The Bishops go beyond concern with their own parishes and Church, when they plead for " a just order, remote from all human caprice, which spreads its protecting hand over the inalienable human rights of men and removes them from the reach of any human force ".

At the end of the document the Bishops state frankly that they "come forward to defend with particular vehemence all those who are unable to plead for their rights themselves: for the young people, for the innocent who are in prison and oppressed, including those who are not of our blood and nationality; for those who have been evacuated and deported; for the workers who are prisoners and of foreign race".

This ardent plea for the imprisoned and the oppressed, the foreign slave workers and the Jews is clearly based on the Catholic conception of a natural law which is binding on all men and inherent in life. The Protestant conception of freedom is definitely not based on the idea of natural law: it is to all appearance less concrete, less striking, less challenging. It is, in a way, pessimistic, almost mystical. It is derived from the Protestant acceptance of suffering as a way to God.

Yet there are divergent views. For instance, Steinbach says (*Anweisung zum Leben,* page 35ff.), we cannot accept suffering as a sure and certain means of attaining eternal life. We are, in reality, never sure whether we shall be accepted after death. Suffering and service are no guarantee of eternity. On the contrary, our task is to attain real freedom by having the courage of our conviction whatever the consequences. Only where there is such freedom, such readiness to sacrifice, can anything good be attained (loc. cit., page 37). We hear also in this context of "freedom as the essence of human life" (loc. cit., page 102).

We find a full explanation of the Protestant attitude and claim to freedom in Karl Barth's *Die Lehre von Gott,* 1942. Freedom is a gift from God, His Law " places man in freedom " (loc. cit., page 650). The essence of this freedom is, in the words of Barth, " peace and joy ". In this way there is a fundamental difference between this divine freedom and whatever human freedom we are granted by the powers that be. For it is the essence of human authorities " to curtail the freedom of man under the pretext of their own divinity, and by pretending that it is only for his own good that they prevent him from being peaceful and full of joy ".

All these human powers are distrustful of man, " it would be too dangerous to set him free ", he would " abuse freedom, would harm himself and others ". We find in Barth the most scathing denunciation of state-power: " They scare man from every angle; they scare him intellectually with the fear of isolation. They scare him by suggesting that he might come off a loser. They scare him morally so that he is afraid of the possibilities of his own nature. They scare him politically so that he is afraid of his own impotence." As against those fears and limitations " the law of God gives freedom to man ". There we find pessimism overcome by a new and overwhelming sense of freedom derived from faith. " God demands that we are free " (loc. cit., page 659).

It seems not without significance that the concern for freedom has entered even into religious writing and preaching in the course of the War. Under the shadow of the swastika the question whether those who have shown courage to plead for freedom have meant freedom for themselves or freedom for others sounds rather hypocritical. Public demands made by Protestant and Catholic alike have mentioned " men of different race and nationality " as people entitled to be free no less than Germans.

Be that as it may, the remarkable feature of this re-emerging free thought is that it shows this deep concern with the problem of freedom for all. While the various attempts to find a solution to the problems of fear and myth are somewhat unevenly divided between various authors and schools, the problem of freedom is common to them all. They all

make a clear and powerful response to the questions they
know to be in the minds of their readers and listeners: What
is freedom? How can it be achieved? How can it be safe-
guarded?

After more than a decade of totalitarian dictatorship it may
seem surprising that this question should be a burning one
for millions of people. What proof is there? Just this—
that there is hardly an important pastoral letter or statement
by Church leaders, hardly an important book by a freedom-
loving secular writer which does not deal with the subject.
The total number of people reached by all these agencies together must run into millions and millions. Obviously these
millions must have asked for it.

Under so immediate and menacing a threat to liberty and
life as that coming from a modern dictatorship, the most
primitive of all forms of freedom, freedom to live, becomes
essential. In various ways this most profound of freedoms
can be and actually has been jeopardized by the unholy
power of the absolute state. *Habeas corpus* has been abol-
ished from the constitution of the state. The state and its
organs—police, secret police, terroristic agencies of all kind
—are " free " to act against all persons, against all freedoms. To do so, they need break no laws: they can act
within the " law " established by the dictator which places
them above the law, if they deem it useful from the point
of view of the régime.

It is plain then that those who publicly demand justice
and the right to life for all men of whatever creed or race
or political opinion challenge the power of such a state.
They take it upon themselves to suffer the impact of this
state-power which may be directed against themselves with
all its boundless terror. It is no longer an academic question
of how much or how little freedom should be allowed. It
simply becomes a question of preserving one's own freedom

to live by remaining silent, or else risking it by demanding this primitive freedom for others. Protests from persons living outside this fateful realm where everything is at stake, however enlightened and idealistic they may be, cannot have the same deadly urgency and courage. Criticisms from outside this deadly circle have little relevance.

Demands for this most essential of all freedoms, freedom of life, have been made on various occasions by leaders of the Fighting Churches in Germany. To quote an instance from a late stage in the War—the Call issued by the Confessional Church in Germany in May 1944 for a " Day of Penitence and Prayer " (quoted in *Spiritual Issues of the War*, October 19th, 1944), we read: "Woe to us and our nation when we make little of the life that God has given, and man, whom God has created in His image, is only assessed as to his utility; when it is considered right to take life because human beings are considered as of no value, or because they belong to another race, when hatred and cruelty are the order of the day—for God says: ' Thou shalt not kill.' "

Another striking example is the letter addressed by Bishop Wurm to members of the Reich Government in the spring of 1943. He demanded " an end to all measures of putting to death members of other nations or races without legal sentence from either civil or military law courts. Such measures have increasingly become known through soldiers home on leave. They weigh on the conscience of all Christian patriots, because they are contrary to God's commandments. The same applies to the practice of disposing of lunatics. These measures will have terrible consequences for our nation."

The letter remained without any effect. So, on July 16th, 1943, a second letter was addressed to all members of the Government. Bishop Wurm protested that all attempts of churchmen to get into touch with the Government or high officials of the state or the party " to bring to their knowledge important concerns of Christian circles in Germany " had failed. " Their written requests were not answered. Their efforts to obtain personal interviews have not been successful."

He went on to point out that this might provide the Christians with an easy alibi. " This might suggest that we may now be silent and avoid any share of responsibility for future happenings. But even under the present political régime every Christian bears his share of the collective responsibility, because he is called to defend what is right and to witness against what is wrong."

Then comes an open attack in almost Biblical and prophetic style: " On behalf of the living as well as the fallen Evangelical Christians of Germany I appeal to the Government of the German Reich, as the oldest Evangelical Bishop representing wide circles of the Evangelical Church: In the name of God, and for the sake of the German nation, we urge the responsible leaders of the Reich to put an end to the persecution and annihilation to which many men and women are subjected without legal sentence within the sphere of German rule.

" Individual incidents give grounds to fear that, after the great majority of non-Aryans within German reach have been annihilated, the so-called ' privileged non-Aryans ', who so far have been spared, will be in danger of the same treatment. We protest particularly urgently against any measures threatening the sacrament of matrimony in legally unimpeachable families, as well as the children resulting from such families." This was an attempt to protect the half-Jews, or Jews who were married to " Aryans " then threatened with annihilation.

But the protest did not stop there. " These intentions,

as well as the measures of annihilation already directed
against other non-Aryans, are in sharpest contradiction to
God's commandments and violate the fundamental principles of all western thought and practice, the divine right
of human existence and human dignity as such.

" We appeal to these divine rights of man," the Bishop
continues, " and we solemnly raise our voice also against
numerous measures taken in occupied territory. Happenings, which have become known in the homeland and are
being much discussed, weigh heavily on the conscience and
strength of innumerable men and women within the German nation." In the middle of the War, then, in summer
1943, when the issue was far from being decided on the
battle-fields, he tells Hitler and his Ministers that " the fact
of some of these measures causes them (innumerable men
and women in Germany) greater suffering than their daily
sacrifices ". He does not deny that there may be the argument of the " hard necessities of war ". But " we are convinced that arbitrary measures directed against life, property
and freedom of religion, such as those carried out by Party
and State, have done infinitely more harm than a possible
misuse of justice and leniency could have done."

The Bishop goes on to proclaim proudly that " up till
to-day German Christendom has stood firm in resisting the
attacks directed against its faith and practice. However, we
deeply deplore the widespread oppression of freedom of religion and conscience, the continuous attempt to decrease
parental and Christian influence in the education of youth,
the detention of perfectly honourable persons in concentration
camps, the undermining of legal practice and the uncertainty
in the realm of law resulting from it." He guards against the
accusation which Nazis were so ready to launch, namely, that
these Christians are only speaking for themselves, that they
only want something for themselves. " While we voice these

concerns in the name of innumerable Christians, we do not demand anything for ourselves. German Evangelical Christendom fully shares the burden of all sacrifices. It does not want any special rights or privileges. It does not aspire to power, nor does it desire might. But nothing and no one in the world shall prevent us from being Christians and from interceding for what is right before God."

This document was passed on to all responsible groups of the German opposition, to all Churches and political parties, to the trade unions and academic people. Obviously Bishop Wurm and his friends were risking their lives. But towards the end of 1943 the threat to all remaining non-Aryans increased, and the danger was imminent that about 400,000 " half-Aryans " would follow the Jews to their death. It was then that the Council of the German Evangelical Church gave Bishop Wurm its full support for a final and forceful protest. The Catholics were drawn into this joint action, and invited to take parallel steps. Again Bishop Wurm wrote to the members of the Government individually, sending them the text of his memorandum (December 1943). After explaining why the anxiety for the non-Aryans had lately increased, he stated:

" On religious and ethical grounds I must declare, in agreement with all positive Christian elements of our nation: As Christians we regard this policy of annihilation directed against Jewry as a deep injustice and fatal for our German nation. Killing without necessity of war and without legal sentence is contrary to God's commandments even in those cases where it is commanded by the authorities. It will sooner or later bring its Nemesis, like every deliberate transgression of God's commandments." As was shown later, the Nazis felt particularly offended by the next sentence: " Our people widely regard the sufferings caused by enemy air action as retribution for what has been done to the Jews.

The burning of houses and churches, the splintering and crushing noises during the night-raids, the escaping from the destroyed houses snatching a few belongings, the helplessness in looking for a place of refuge, painfully remind the population of what the Jews have had to suffer on earlier occasions."

In spring 1944, a letter from the Government arrived, in which Wurm was threatened with arrest and " grave measures " if he continued. In that case, the letter said, he could not be spared any longer in spite of having suffered the loss of his sons, who had fallen at the front. If he continued to refer to " God's visitations and judgments " in his utterances and public sermons, as he had done so far, this would be regarded as " unbearable defeatism ", with all the consequences which the Reich was not hesitant to bring on less prominent and younger men. Any reply from his side was forbidden. Consequently, Bishop Wurm asked one of his collaborators to reply on his behalf. The reply was that he would neither alter his attitude nor his actions.

His life was spared—apparently for a number of reasons. He had become the most prominent of the Evangelical leaders, and Hitler hesitated to antagonize the Protestants outright. Furthermore, he was already very old—seventy-five. He had also lost his sons in the War. But, while he escaped unhurt, some of his friends and collaborators lost their lives. Some were sent to the front with the obvious intention of getting rid of them there. Others were sent to concentration camps. Others were shot by the Gestapo. For there were a number of men who were either themselves leaders of the political opposition, or else in touch with them. Amongst those who were shot by the Gestapo was Pastor Bonhoeffer. The Gestapo shot him shortly before the Americans arrived and liberated the concentration camp in which he was held.

From the point of view of the future it is vital that this plea, and others of a similar kind, should have been made. It is vital that these Protestants should have protested. It is vital that they should "confess with contrite hearts: We Christians are guilty of sharing in neglect and disregard of the Divine commands. We have often remained silent, have said too little, or have been too timid to stand up for our conviction that God's commandments apply to us and our time."

We find the same spirit prevailing in the words of the Joint Pastoral Letter of the Catholic Bishops (October 1943): "The slaughter of people who have no personal guilt is in itself evil, even when it is ostensibly carried out in the interest of the common good, as, for example, against the mortally wounded, against new-born infants with inherited disease, unfitted for life, against innocent hostages and unarmed prisoners of war, against men of other races and origin." Here we find clearly established the antithesis between the freedom to live and the claim of the dictatorship to take life "ostensibly in the interest of the common good". Here we find upheld that most primitive right of man, the right to preserve his own individual life against all claims of an impersonal, uncontrollable "common good". "No single point on the map of a life worthy of man is beyond the line of good or evil."

Elementary Freedom

The same statement defines the method by which this elementary freedom can be established not only objectively, but also subjectively. Objectively, it is established simply as the right of the individual to preserve his own life, whatever his political, national, racial origin or allegiance. " The

Government can and must only punish with death criminals who have merited it." Only individual acts of crime against life can deprive an individual of the right, of the freedom, to live.

Subjectively, this Christian plea establishes conscience as the reliable guide to the problems of life and freedom. " The stars of the conscience illuminate all latitudes of life. No stretch of land shown on its territory is foreign to the conscience, to the law which reflects it—not even politics or commerce or public life."

This freedom to live is, therefore, maintained even against claims of economic, political or social expediency or so-called necessities. These Christian leaders do not accept the case of those who would tolerate loss of life through economic distress, through starvation, or similar causes. Neither do they accept the plea that political reasons, or reasons of " public welfare " or, perhaps, of public opinion, may have prompted actions which resulted in the loss of life of innocent persons. It is important for the future to see these guiding principles, which constitute a clear delineation of the duties of the citizen and of the state towards the elementary freedom to live.

Furthermore, there is a powerful reply to the common argument—common particularly under the pressure of a totalitarian régime—that there are fields, such as foreign policy economics, civics, where the knowledge and the insight of the individual may be inadequate to justify his opposition against the actions of his Government. It has been a frequent excuse in modern states that " I know too little about it to say anything ". This excuse is not accepted. For here we find a criterion introduced which is quite different from that which is commonly upheld as the most comfortable excuse. Usually the argument turns on "knowledge ": " I know too little." " I cannot see the merits of the case." And similar such excuses. They are the daily bread of political, or rather unpolitical, life in a totalitarian state.

Here, then, is a demand which does not accept this argument at all. It does not enter into a discussion about knowledge and insight and information. It reduces the issue of freedom to the most elementary issue, namely, the issue of conscience. The individual is told clearly and inescapably that this is not a matter of argument, but a matter of conscience. He is told that each individual of whatever race, nationality, faith, has the right to live. Whenever, or wherever, he is deprived of this right a crime is committed. For the onlooker, the " merits of the case " are beside the point. It is not a question of such impersonal things as " economic distress " or " political necessity " or whatever excuses the authorities may produce. It is merely a question of conscience. " Thou shalt not kill " is an eternal law, which he finds deeply rooted not only in the laws of God, but also in his or her own conscience. When this law is violated, the conscience is violated. Action on the part of all individuals who act according to their conscience becomes a necessity.

It is characteristic of the elementary nature of this public discussion about the freedom of man that leaders of the most varied kinds—Christians and humanists, romantics and realists, fall back on this last and vital criterion, namely, the human conscience. The outstanding example is Grisebach's *Schicksalsfrage des Abendlandes*, which forces the student to doubt every dogma, every historical fact, every method, and every theory, until and unless his conscience drives him to adopt it. He singles out the freedom of religion as the outstanding example of freedom, and he comes to the conclusion that even this freedom is bound to lead to new enslavements of the mind unless it is controlled by the human conscience (loc. cit., page 152).

Grisebach differentiates freedom of religion from freedom of conscience. Freedom of conscience is demanded by the conscience of free men. " It is an eternal law to correct oneself and to overcome mistakes which one has made." The utmost he is prepared to concede is " freedom of conscience side by side with freedom of religion "/(loc. cit., page 153). He believes it is necessary to maintain freedom of conscience in order to prevent religious, or pseudo-religious institutions enslaving the human mind with superimposed dogmas. He sees in this freedom the very source of Protestantism.

It is important to realize why Grisebach and others like him have insisted on this scepticism in the course of this war. It is not that they wished to guard against God or against eternal laws. God and eternal laws are there: but between them and the human individual all sorts of dogmas and false authorities, demands and theories are constantly being erected which threaten the freedom of the very mind which they claim to uphold. Grisebach becomes very explicit, almost political, when he says: " If there were a complete freedom of religion—as against freedom of conscience—every individual, every nation, every class could claim the right to establish its own religion, to create its own religion."

Freedom of Conscience

This view takes the extreme form of giving up the claim for freedom of religion as far as Christianity is concerned. The argument is based on the insistence that for the individual Christian the relationship between man and God is a direct one, unaffected by dogmas, organizations, historical heritages. For him only this direct relationship matters. To claim " freedom of religion " means merely a claim to estab-

lish his Church, and through his Church, to partake in that
greater freedom, the freedom of conscience. This approach is
typical of many for whom the question of freedom has become vital. It does not necessarily deny freedom of religion.
They do not say there should be no freedom of religion.
But, in a situation in which both freedoms, the freedom of
religion and the freedom of conscience are endangered, the
philosopher and teacher tells his students: "Concentrate
on the most essential one—freedom of conscience. Do not
waste time and energy, do not let yourself be led astray by
the minor problem of freedom of and for religions. Be true
to yourself and concentrate on following your conscience.
Insist on this most essential freedom of conscience."

Clearly a student of such a text-book, published in 1942,
would be radical in his understanding of what ethics, Christianity, truth would demand from him. He would not get lost
in a struggle for religious privilege. At the same time, there
is no doubt that as soon as new opportunities for the re-
organization of state and society, for the replacement of the
totalitarian order by a more democratic system appeared,
he would advocate, amongst other things, freedom of religion.

This differentiation between freedom of conscience and
freedom of religion corresponds to a radical rediscovery of
what freedom means. Freedom appears as an extremely
complex fact. It is not just a word, a slogan, an easily
framed and easily uttered catch-word. For these thinkers
it has become a vital problem. It has become so real, so
much alive, so precious that they have begun to distinguish
the more essential from the less essential elements in it.
They have learned so much about the limitation of freedom,
they have experienced so cruelly how easily freedom can
be lost, in part or altogether, that they have begun to think:
what are those sections and parts of it which no man can
do without?

In this way Grisebach himself arrives at a completely different sector of the vast problem of freedom, when he says that freedom means the necessity and the right to work. The last part of his book is exclusively devoted to the ethical foundations of work (loc. cit., page 300ff.). As is only logical, he comes to the conclusion that the conditions of work can, in the last analysis, be measured by the conscience of the individual and the community. If we ask our conscience whether and how far conditions of labour, of leisure time, of income, are humane, we arrive at any rate at certain negative limitations. We shall be able to say what is not humane. In this way we are able to say what is not freedom. . . .

Freedom and Power

There is, of course, much direct discussion of freedom in the political sense as well as all this. Even the old historian Friedrich Meinecke, the protagonist of the historical school, comes to the conclusion that without freedom and without roots in the soil of the nation we are not even able to understand history (*Vom Geschichtlichen Sinn und vom Sinn der Geschichte,* 1939). He sees freedom as a necessity for a healthy national and international development. He finds one of the reasons for the breakdown in the spiritual stability and political and historical sobriety of the Germans in the shock which they have received through the First World War, and in the loss of certain freedoms in consequence of it. He finds that loss of freedom and humiliation leave a sting in the soul of a nation which affects even its ability to see objectively. His diagnosis of the present period arrives at the conclusion that Germany has been in a state of crisis ever since 1914, and that the revolution of 1933 merely began a new stage of this crisis. In this sense it is a crisis of freedom just as much as it is a crisis of a nation (loc. cit., page 132f.).

But his definition of freedom does not remain altogether political. He finds freedom as the logical consequence of reason (loc. cit., page 80), he sees that freedom " destroys the bonds of illusion and ignorance " (loc. cit., page 81). He finds that "all virtues grow, all trades increase, the arts flourish as the consequence of freedom " (loc. cit., page 77). As if the great tradition of idealism would claim its right in the education of this new and grimly endangered genera-tion, men like Meinecke have broken their silence and de-fined such vital issues as that of freedom in its various forms and consequences.

An even louder and clearer voice has been heard from Munich where Alfred von Martin (*Nietzsche und Burckhardt*) explains the relationship, and in many ways the antagonism between freedom and power. He goes even further, and finds that the civilization of Europe may finally be decided by the answer which the Europeans give to this challenge of how to combine, how to balance freedom and power (loc. cit., page 151).

Martin underlines that great liberal thinker Burckhardt's determined will to freedom, a will which is not prepared to give way to, and even demands the reassertion of freedom against the arbitrariness of absolutisms of all kind. " Burck-hardt does not deny that Napoleon like Michelangelo had genius. But even against genius he wants to remain a free man.' He does not tolerate superhuman power, which oppresses all human freedom and may be not even great-ness, but merely power—as in the case of Louis XIV or Napoleon " (loc. cit., page 152). It need hardly be men-tioned that in these works, where the scholar becomes a political fighter, the examples quoted are unimportant, but the ideas expounded all-important. If proof were needed

Martin provides it in the following passage (loc. cit., page 153):

"Burckhardt is conscious of a supreme duty towards an idea which is greater than any genius—the idea of Europe. The individual, however important he may be as a personality, has to be judged according to the degree to which he has served or damaged that idea. The idea of Europe is: freedom, restraint, and humanity."

There is a militant note in this plea. Martin glorifies the Wars of Liberation of 1813, not because they have become the beginning of modern nationalism in Germany, but, on the contrary, because they sprang from the supra-national faith in the justice of a war "against the arrogant tyrant". He deliberately uses the words which Blücher wrote to his wife in October 1813. He also quotes Arndt's explanation of the victory of Leipzig: "We are free. We breathe again." He explains freedom, also national freedom, as an ethical good (loc. cit., page 157). But he goes right into politics when he finds that "the idea of a world-monarchy as expounded by Napoleon is the expression of an absolutism which does not recognize any limitations and frontiers"; against this "revolutionary romanticism" Burckhardt regards Talleyrand's policy of the balance of power and his antagonism to the hegemony of one power as "an interest of European freedom", as an expression of "political reason", and Martin upholds his aim (loc. cit., page 159). In this way the idea of freedom is applied to the immediate international situation and it necessarily leads to an attack against the Hitlerite idea of a continental hegemony by "an arrogant tyrant".

A liberal voice in praise of a great liberal European was also raised in the middle of the War. Karl Vossler, the great Munich Professor and writer on romance literature, published an appreciation of his friend Benedetto Croce, on the latter's seventieth birthday on February 25th, 1936, and re-published it in Volume IV of his collection of essays, *Aus der Romanischen Welt*, in 1942. There we find the brilliant summing-up: " Neither catastrophes of whatever kind, nor errors, inadequacies, signs of dejection amongst his friends have ever been able to shatter his faith in the supremacy of the spirit and in the development of human freedom " (loc. cit., page 136). The supremacy of the spirit and the development of human freedom are the ideals which have been kept alive by men like Croce when not only their enemies, but even their friends, who " showed signs of dejection " threatened to shatter this faith.

Response of Youth

The manifesto of the Munich students who revolted in 1943 could hardly be regarded as a work of art or learning, in the sense in which those terms apply to the words we have been considering, but there seems to have been a deep connection between the appeal of these students and the writings of scholars. We know that a Professor of Psychology, Huber, was amongst those who were executed by the Third Reich, and that those undergraduates, led by the Scholls, who followed his teachings, paid with their lives for it. In their very moving appeal we find again the praise of freedom, " our most precious possession of which Adolf Hitler's state has cheated us ".

The academic style, the pure idealism of the older leaders, gives way here to the flaming words of the young political pamphleteers. They are cynically, realistically clear about the many meanings, the easy abuses to which the word " freedom " can be reduced. They know that even the totalitarian state is only too ready to use it in order to win over the loyalty of freedom-seeking masses. Therefore they write: "Freedom and honour! For ten years these two fine words have been abused, debased and distorted by Hitler and his clique." This is no longer the language of those who live in a world of their own in which high ideals have lost none of their splendour, though they may occasionally be overshadowed by threats and defections from outside. No, these students and their leaders have translated the language of the masters into a language of fighters.

"What freedom and honour really means for them (the Nazis), of this they have given more than enough proof in a decade of destroying every vestige of material and spiritual liberty, every moral substance within the German people. Even the dumbest of Germans must have had their eyes opened by the terrible blood-bath which, in the name of freedom and honour, they have inflicted on the whole of Europe."

There is no resignation, although there is full realization of the manifold uses to which this one precious word of freedom can be put. There is a challenge to those who want to abuse it. Without any theoretical explanations, with a direct and immediate kind of action, these students hold on to the very words which they have shown up in their distortion inside the totalitarian framework. "Our people are ready to rise against the enslavement of Europe through Nazism, ready to rise for a real and rejuvenated faith in freedom and honour!" (Quoted from the translation in *Germany's Road to Democracy,* page 77f.).

The same words which are branded as the catchwords of the oppressive régime are torn out of their false context and used as they stand as the slogan for popular action. Yes, this is thought which is nearer to action than to deliberation —an altogether rare, too rare example of political literature written under the shadow of the swastika during the Second

World War. As a piece of political action it constitutes in itself a remarkable guide to the realization of freedom. For it is obvious that the entire fact of freedom, even as a thought and an ideal, is bound to remain unreal unless the student is taught how to get hold of it, how to realize it. Political action of a revolutionary nature is one of the methods, but frequently, if not, alas, mostly, a way which remains barred by the power of the state machine. The easy and flaming antithesis which is so characteristic of this political approach remains dependent upon chances of putting it into practice. They are mostly lacking. Power to carry these convictions through, to publish them, is lacking. The totalitarian monster is on guard against flaming words like these! Therefore, powerful though this method is, it often comes to nothing.

Freedom in Pure Thought

As the War went on a growing number of people sought relief from the oppressive world around them in the realm of the spirit. As often in history a world of freedom grew in the remote and isolated study of the lonely thinker or artist, and he found his public in similarly lonely homes all over the country. This was more than mere escapism. It was a question of relative values. Things spiritual and artistic gained in importance the longer the terror outside went on. There is an esoteric kind of freedom in a beautiful poem, in a perfectly balanced sonata, in a penetrating work of science or philosophy.

Such works, written even in the course of the War, were strongholds of freedom for millions of individuals for whom freedom as a physical reality appeared far away, altogether outside their reach. Novels like those of Wiechert, Carossa, poems like those of Carossa or the younger Jünger, studies like those of Smend, Brandi, Vossler or Andreas, dozens of them, find their place here.

In addition, and even more important in extent and penetrating power, there were the classics. The demand for and the understanding of classical works of literature and music acquired an almost desperate urgency.

These aspects of freedom had, of course, little or no political significance. But man must regain freedom for himself, in his own mind and soul, before contemplating how he can achieve it in state and society. Without being absolutely clear about the essence and meaning of freedom you cannot fight for it. Or if you start fighting without knowing what it is about you may easily set up a new form of slavery in place of the old one.

The educational process referred to, therefore, was a necessary foundation for later actions. This holds good of many diverse activities, such as study groups, based on books like those of Martin or Grisebach; reading circles devoted to poetry, or religion; play-readings carried on in many a private house and even in remote corners of camps or workshops— the plays chosen being mainly classics which could easily be obtained and would not raise suspicions. But there were plays amongst them, such as those of Schiller, Büchner and Shakespeare, which have lost none of their revolutionary appeal.

There is no doubt that in the minds of many of these authors, teachers and writers a primary purpose of their gallant work was to train people in freedom of thought and, ultimately, for freedom. Some of these writings show clearly that they are meant not only to add to free thought, but also to show how freedom may be achieved. There is a clear realization of the facts, often ignored, that freedom, whether as an ideal, or in practice, has to be learned and can be forgotten. The individual and the group may feel the need, the urge to be free, but they may be incapable of acting on it. That is why we find Grisebach's work divided into question and answer. The untrained student can find the questions he is interested in stated as the basis of the entire treatise. A hundred and thirty questions—instead of 130 paragraphs which would be natural in a "free" academic society—are put and answered. It is a crude but effective way of training students in the technique of free thought.

But there is more to it than this. Ernst Jünger remarks (*Auf den Marmorklippen*, 1939) that man finds the eternal in the laws inherent in nature and whatever else he studies. In such study we can realize the "power of science" as a source of freedom, of that essential freedom of the mind. Even the form and structure of a little flower can be a source of strength against the powers of destruction (loc. cit., page 95).

There is a method of attaining this freedom of the mind through work. Jünger praises work of this kind—devoted, intensive work, which is something by no means confined to the scientist or scholar, but inherent in all true effort. He praises it as a source of freedom, as an antidote against the destructive power of the totalitarian state. "If we do our jobs in this way, we human beings feel somehow endowed with special powers. It is strange that we are then soon seized by a feeling of increased freedom." He compares this influence of work on the individual who is in danger with the increased feeling of security which the soldier at the front feels if he throws himself into his job. There is a militant note in these attitudes of the worker and of the soldier, a somewhat irrational feeling that one road to freedom leads through their work; perhaps through their service to the community.

This recognition is remarkable also in so far as it points

to one of the major reasons for the unbroken spirit of freedom amongst the working classes and the peasants. Obviously it would be too simple an explanation to be the sole reason. But it can hardly be accidental that thousands of workers and peasants with only a minimum of theoretical and intellectual armour have not abandoned either their claim or their hope for freedom, even though it remained, for the most part, secret. It seems that from this working together they derived a feeling of strength which became the source of inextinguishable love of freedom.

III. MYTHS, FAITH AND REASON

CONTEMPORARY thought has become increasingly aware of the influence of mystical and para-mystical elements ever since the rise of Nazism to power in 1933. It is a problem by no means confined to Germany. Huxley's *Grey Eminence* is an example of one modern approach to it.

There is a difference, however, between the issue as it strikes the western democrat and the issue as it appears under the totalitarian system. A certain range of facts in the totalitarian state are beyond reasoning. The "leader" is more than a political head, more than a human being, he is absolute, he is a "principle", *das Führerprinzip*. The acceptance of this leadership-principle introduces an element of the mystical into the life of the community. More than that, the mystical becomes the mythical. And then reason, even though not incompatible with the mystical, becomes dangerous and revolutionary. The follower of the modern myth reacts almost instinctively against the cold, hard logic of reason and objectivity.

The antagonism between these principles—reason and myth—developed more vehemently than ever during the War. Prior to 1939, the situation was still apparently fluid. After Hitler's victories in Europe the issue became perfectly clear. From then onwards the intelligentsia realized that the whole burden of decision between reason and myth rested on them. It is remarkable how this pressure of the historical situation shook many out of their apathy and escapism.

Health and Truth

Take, for instance, the doctor who is interested, not in
58

theory but in practical human affairs! How is he, how is anybody who has to deal with human suffering and human problems, to behave in a community regulated by laws which belong to an abstract philosophy of life, or by commands which derive from irrational myth? (Victor von Weizsäcker, *Arzt und Kranker,* 1941.)

The reply is remarkable (loc. cit., page 177ff.). For it takes into consideration the multitude of orders and laws, of regulations and principles, which purport to form modern communities. He enumerates leadership, family, relationship between parents and children, marriage, state, sexual relations, but "also the primitive forms of community relations, such as hatred, love, will, reason and their importance for the relationship between the patient and the doctor".

We find, Weizsäcker concludes, that the multitude of problems is overwhelming. We cannot honestly say that we see a clear theoretical way through them giving direction to practical action if we are faced with human suffering and need. He is even sceptical about "a formal, abstract moral philosophy, such as the Kantian ethics, which requires you to treat a patient as you would wish to be treated" (loc. cit., page 178). The reason for this scepticism even towards rational and ethical principles as well as mythical orders is inherent in the totalitarian situation. For there we find it postulated that certain categories of men are good, others are bad, certain races or classes are human, others are not. Consequently ethical standards are applicable only to a section of mankind or of the community.

The conclusion which is drawn from this dilemma is the plain negation of all abstract claims as irrelevant to those who want to alleviate suffering. "Therefore I believe that there is little room here for ethics based on purpose or laws, but only for ethics based on love, appearing in actions of love, without appealing to anybody" (loc. cit., page 178).

This appeal for an approach which is really beyond the antagonism between realism and mysticism does not, however, shirk the dilemma as it has appeared in the modern community. "The formation of the community is carried on between the Scylla of realism with its tendency of diminishing love, and the Charybdis of love with its tendency towards irrationalization. Without any doubt a generation is growing up which can bear a degree of rationalization and mechanization which would have deprived the youth of my own and older generations of their belief in spiritual values and in love" (loc. cit., page 178).

This analysis acknowledges that what is called "a romantic attitude" (*romantische Seelenlage*) tends to overstress the antagonism between realism and love. It admits that realism and love are not necessarily incompatible, but that their inherent antagonism makes it a continuous task to combine them in action (loc. cit., page 179). There is a revolutionary sound in the confession of a doctor of the Third Reich: "I do not believe in the so-called 'love for the cause', love for rational action, which I think is the pitcher which goes so often to the well that it comes home broken at last. I believe in love for men."

In order to realize the revolutionary quality of this confession it is necessary to remember that the dividing line between reason and myth, between realism and mysticism, has become dim and uncertain under the overwhelming power of the totalitarian state. For rationalism is an approach to matters which our mind delineates as facts, as figures, as values. Rationalism in one age does not necessarily mean rationalism in another age. To approach a matter "rationally" means something different, say, in medieval society and in modern democratic society. Nothing could show this more clearly than the very field which Weizsäcker is exploring anew, namely the field of human approach to suffering and disease. To kill mentally diseased persons was a thing which barbarian civilizations considered " rational ", just as the Nazi state has done. The question which the individual, or the doctor, has to answer is obviously not whether the killing of mental patients is " rational " or not, but whether it is " good " or not. There may be arguments as to what is " rational " in such a case or, say, under difficult military circumstances when nutrition is endangered by a blockade. To put it bluntly, when England's supplies were endangered by the U-boats in 1940 and 1941 the feeding of incurable persons might have appeared " irrational " from the point of view of national defence. But not to feed them, or rather to kill them, would have been just as much murder as under other circumstances. It would have been " bad ", " immoral ", a " sin ", but it may have been possible, under certain circumstances, to defend it as " rational ".

The crisis in thought and values inside Germany developed to such an extent that the medical man could no longer avoid these issues. And he found that the issue was not between " rational " and " irrational ", but between " human " and " inhuman ", between love and myths—even myths clothed in practical advantage or faith. In the last resort " health and truth become the same " (loc. cit., page 179).

The Catholic Approach

The view we have been considering resembles the Christian position in regard to modern myths, only the Christian point of view is determined by faith. The Joint Pastoral Letter of the German Bishops (October 1943) insists on the First Commandment, and quotes it in full. From there the Bishops proceed to an open denunciation of " elegant idols set up in the imagination of men of culture who are in-

different to truth.   They all call the visions and dreams con-
jured up by their mythical poetry ' the divine '."

In this statement we find the fighting Catholic Church
standing up against " culture " as an expression of national
self-worship, and of the revival of ancient pagan dreams.
But this decision has a greater claim upon the faithful than
any purely private decision on some unavoidable issue in
public life.   " Religion is not just a private matter, to be
brought forth only behind the barred door of the individual's
private chamber.   It is a public force which exists by virtue
of the universality and world-wide obligation of .its truth,
moral bases, and values.   A man cannot be a Christian only
in the silence of his inner life and a heathen in his outward
life."

The Christian position is thus logical, if not rational:
a logical denunciation.   Furthermore, it is an open appeal,
and an appeal for an open stand against the various expressions of these modern myths.   But this is by no means
the only example which can be quoted.   Count Galen, Bishop
of Münster, has gone into this strange field where myth
and reality clash, in his Lenten Pastoral Letter in 1944:

" It is true, there are still a great number of people who
have never bent their knees before the power of this state.
But there is no denying the fact that the number of those who
do not listen to God in their public, professional, social and
even private life is very great.   They find followers and imi-
tators and henchmen even amongst those who still call themselves Christians.   The public life of very wide circles of the
one-time Christian peoples of Europe has drifted away from
the Christian truths.   Technical progress and the domination
over the forces of nature have reached a climax; it has become the highest purpose in the life of many."

Again, this attack on the dogma of the modern totalitarian myth is " realistic " in that the answer of a Christian

based on Christian truths is based on realities. This becomes clearer still in Galen's subsequent interpretation of
this war as God's warning to man: " God speaks to-day in
the only language to which mankind still listens—through the
thunder of battles, the noise of propellers, the explosion of
bombs. He speaks to us through the very forces which He
has created, in which He has instilled those laws which our
scientists have discovered and our inventors have enlisted
in the service of death and destruction. In the voice of this
murderous war, of death and devastation everywhere, God,
calls to man: I am the Lord. Man thought he could free
himself from God, he hoped for an entirely carefree existence
through the technical mastery of nature, he thought God had
become superfluous. To-day God answers this challenge.
In total war the proud inventions become weapons of destruction and of death. Everywhere smouldering ruins! Do you
realize how mistaken all your calculations have been? "

This interpretation, amongst many similar ones, re-
presents probably the most " realistic " approach to the
mythology of the totalitarian state. Its terminology and its
style are technical, modern, realistic, not Biblical and anti-
quated as many of the others are. It interprets the totalitarian state as the final expression of paganism, this war as
the final expression of totalitarianism, its characteristics as
" death, destruction . . . murder . . . devastation ". It reduces
the modern myths to their most essential elements: " Everywhere smouldering ruins." That is the symbol of this " new
order ".

There are other similar statements, such as the Lenten
Pastoral Letter of the Archbishop of Freiburg, Dr. Gröber,
who declares: " Having become godless, men hope to initiate
a new cultural epoch, which deprives man of his likeness to
God and is satisfied with a pedigree which has its origins
only in the animal kingdom. The *Herrenmensch* who

thus comes into existence is fundamentally an animal which stands upright and is decked out in suitable clothes. A blond beast, and nothing more." (Cf. *Left News*, May, 1944.)

As early as July 1941 Bishop Galen placed the issue squarely before the Christians of Germany. "With State bureaucracy comes danger to freedom of thought and action —and the more so, when the State expresses ideals hostile to Christianity and tries to force these same ideals upon the people. Particularly is the danger hard for those who are employed by the State, and what courage and heroism is required by such State employees to profess themselves" (*German Home Front*, page 259).

The Protestant Approach

The issues involved were no less clearly defined by Protestants belonging to the fighting section of Protestantism. The first great pronouncement was made on May 31st, 1934, in Barmen. We mention this so-called Barmen declaration here because it has constituted the generally accepted rule for the Confessional Church ever since, and whatever forms of expression the individual theologian or pastor may have found, this Barmen declaration has acted and proved its power as the golden rule. The first thesis of the Barmen declaration ends with a clear definition of the Christian approach to life as against the totalitarian myth. "We denounce the false dogma that the Church can or must acknowledge as a source of its teachings, outside and alongside the word of God, other events and powers, personalities or truths, as revelations of God" (Karl Barth, *Die Lehre von Gott*, 1940, page 194).

These "other events" were, in the Third Reich for instance, Hitler's access to power. How often has Hitler himself pointed to his spectacular rise to power as a " mystical " sign of God's will, as a revelation of God's intention.   As late as summer 1944 the failure of von Stauffenberg's brave assassination-attempt was widely interpreted as the expression of the will of God by Hitler's followers.   The Christian reply to all such attempts to create modern myths is contained in the Barmen statement's rejection of " other powers, personalities and truths ", or rather pseudo-truths, which appeared in Germany along with the Third Reich.

Karl Barth explains clearly and fully that the Barmen declaration was the result of the new situation in which the Church " was confronted with the myth of the totalitarian state, at first slightly disguised, but soon enough undisguised " (loc. cit., page 195).

In 1936 we find this irreconcilable antagonism to the totalitarian myth expressed in a memorandum which the leaders of the Confessional Church handed to Hitler. Again, we mention this memorandum because it has retained its political and theological importance right through the War, and was incorporated in many a sermon in the course of the War.   " When blood, race, nationality, and honour are regarded as eternal values, the first Commandment obliges the Christian to refuse this valuation.   When the Aryan is glorified, the Word of God teaches that all men are sinful."

The most cruel and crucial aspect of this modern myth is openly challenged in the words: " If the Christian is forced by the anti-Semitism of the Nazi *Weltanschauung* to hate the Jews, he is on the contrary bidden by the Christian commandment to love his neighbour " (*German Home Front,* page 284).

A direct reply to the challenge of modern myth was published in 1938 by Eberhard Müller, a Protestant pastor in Berlin.   There we find an analysis of modern myths which seems to go far towards laying bare their essential roots.

Myth is the result of fear, it is an attempt " to master life by clouding the reality of death " (*Verstandenes Dogma,* page 140). Müller recognizes the reality of death as one of the deepest motive-powers in human existence. He insists that the Bible, and particularly the great thinkers of the Old Testament, are quite clear about the fear of death, which is natural and human but "makes man a slave ". But he warns against that ancient Germanic myth, the " religious transfiguration of Walhalla ". He goes so far as to state that "modern myth has maintained that man lives on in the divine force of the nation " (loc. cit., page 141). This, in the opinion of Protestantism, is the real issue between myth and faith—or, indeed, between myth and reality. Is there a "mystical" survival in Walhalla, or in the nation? Is there a " mystical " way out of the always present antagonism between life and death? Or is there only death in all its darkness and life in all its vigour, and above everything God? The Christian reply to these myths is God, " from whom comes both the unbroken joy and fulfilment of life, and the brutal recognition of inescapable death " (loc. cit., page 143).

Here we come to one of the major developments inside Germany since 1938-39. The supra-natural—whether myth for some or faith for others—has become an important factor in the consciousness of the people. Serious studies have begun to deal with this problem and to find answers to the growing claims of the Nazi myth. In so doing modern Protestant writers—and indeed Christians generally—have emphasized the supra-natural events and revelations in Christian writings and in the Bible much more than most Christian writers of the nineteenth century. Thus Ernst Steinbach, a soldier who is also a Christian, stresses the reality of miracle in his war-time meditations (*Anweisung zum Leben,* page 157).

Steinbach differentiates between miracles which are miracles because they exist in the mind of man, and miracles which are "objectively recognizable events which carry the stamp of breaking all known natural laws" (loc. cit., page 159). In order to illustrate the first type of "miracles" he quotes the case of a child who runs into the street when a car is approaching at high speed. The child falls, and seems already lost, and then—the car passes it without hurting it. Steinbach concludes that for some people this may seem a happy chance, for others a miracle. It would thus be a miracle or not, according to the mind and soul of the people who witnessed the event.

But he maintains that there are passages in the Bible which describe events which definitely break the known laws of nature; for instance, the story of Jesus walking on the water. The rationalistic interpretation of these stories is that they are partly poetic imaginations of the writers, partly misunderstandings of Jesus' true thoughts and deeds. They offend our ethical and religious consciousness. He follows Kierkegaard in doubting whether God would make the decision easy for man by revealing His power through sheer miracles. The doubt rests on rational, ethical, and religious ground. If God could and would break the laws of nature He would destroy the order which He Himself has given the world. "The question whether there are miracles is not a scientific, but an ethical question" (loc. cit., page 162). At the same time: "If it were possible to prove the existence of God scientifically . . . the way to heaven would be crammed in no time by place-hunters and that rabble which always senses where its bread is buttered and would do everything one asks if it saw an advantage in it."

This discussion whether God reveals His intention in miracles has gained wider importance in face of the increasing claims made on the loyalty of the people by Hitler and his followers because of Hitler's "miraculous" successes. These successes, the totalitarian myth claimed, were the revelation of God's purpose. They were a kind of miracle showing that Hitler was God's chosen instrument.

The Christian Humanistic Approach

But, alas, this does not bring us any nearer understanding that extraordinary phenomenon of our time, the increasing longing of great masses of people for the supra-natural. This longing can be seen in many countries and constitutes in itself nothing peculiar to Fascism or totalitarianism. The power and prestige of the Churches increased during the War on both sides of the front. In totalitarian countries it can only partly be explained as the result of the open opposition of the Fighting Churches to the impact of totalitarianism. In part, it certainly also comes from the deep longing of suffering mankind for religion. In England, for instance, the National Days of Prayer found hundreds of churches filled by vast masses of people which the Church leaders themselves had not expected. In England, too, there was the striking example of Air-Marshal Dowding, the victor of the Battle of Britain, publishing a spiritualistic book. In Germany this development was even more marked because the totalitarian state tried to develop its own myth. Myth there stood in opposition to faith, totalitarian claims clashed with genuine belief. The more serious-minded thinkers and writers found themselves therefore compelled to take account of conflicting claims of myth, faith and reason on a growing section of the community.

It is, therefore, not surprising that myth and reason, myth and faith have been written and talked about a good deal. The Christian approach to the problem is by no means the only one. The humanists have had profound things to say, too. We find authors like Alfred von Martin standing between the Christian and the humanistic camps, or rather on the road to an attempted synthesis between the two. In his great work of 1941, *Nietzsche und Burckhardt,* he pleads for the combination of humanism and Christianity (loc. cit., page 128). He underlines Burckhardt's ideal of " platonic teachings and the modern spirit coinciding with reminiscences of medieval mysticism, dogmatic Christianity, and a monastic outlook ". Here, then, we are confronted with a completely new type of mysticism which is neither bowing before the totalitarian myth, nor expressing itself in the framework of the Church. It is a humanistic Christianity, or rather a Christian humanism. It flourished chiefly in Southern Germany—Martin himself being a professor at Munich University. In a way it is a development of Catholic feeling, but a Catholicism which has turned secular and, in a deep sense, liberal. It is no longer Catholicism; it is, indeed, humanism turning towards a mystical unification of Christian, Greek, Platonic, humanistic, and monastic principles and tendencies.

Whether we call this Christian humanism or humanistic mysticism, it stands in open opposition to the totalitarian myth. Martin finds a formula, almost a declaration of war against this modern myth. " The humanistic ideal means that man shall be in the highest sense a *human* being, not a beast and not a super-man " (loc. cit., page 128f.).

Martin is at the same time conscious of the precariousness of this position. It is a very subtle balance between mysticism and enlightenment which he is striking. Its forcefulness derives chiefly from the quality of the more outstanding representatives of this school, and then from their common antagonist, the totalitarian myth. At the same time there is a deep awareness of the historic dangers of mysticism, and, in particular, of German mysticism. Strange though it may seem, and obviously not without connection with Martin's Roman Catholic origin, he points out a line of development leading from the medieval mystic Eckhardt to Luther and, finally, to Nietzsche. " Finally " is probably the wrong word. This development springs from the intense personal, even individualistic religious feeling, the tendency to seek God and truth in a mystical boundlessness which these men have in common even though they are so different—Eckhardt, the Dominican from the Rhineland, Luther, the Protestant from Saxony, and Nietzsche, the modern philosopher who wrote *The Anti-Christ*. The fact that this school of Christian humanists is able to see a direct connection between medieval mysticism, Protestantism, and Nietzsche as " the radical Protestant who protests against all Churches including the Christian humanistic ethics " (loc. cit., page 234) shows the strength of their own conviction. And part of their conviction is the consciousness of their Hellenic and Roman heritage of form and measure, of a universal system of law and ethics, as against " the individual, revolutionary, protesting " line. Of course, this approach, this stand is not without its own tradition. Martin can point to Troeltsch, to an essay by R. Lindemann in *Hochland*, the leading journal of the Catholics in pre-Hitler Germany, and to other references.

There is a Christian humanistic approach which refuses to build on the traditions of Hellas and Rome. It is rationalistic in the extreme, and looks upon all attempts to cloud the purely rationalistic attitude with profound suspicion. There we find only contempt for anything even faintly resembling myths. Even the historical school, which seeks to " draw lessons from history ", is brushed aside as a camouflaged myth. Eberhard Grisebach's *Schicksalsfrage des Abendlandes* (Bern-Leipzig, 1942) is almost violent in its denunciations of the attempt " to turn history into a myth " (loc. cit., page 139). His reasoning is simple: " It can be of no use to us to learn what place our ancestors have once held, what they have done at that town or in that time. For if we merely imitate them in a difficult situation we may simply act foolishly. Our behaviour in our time is merely endangered by a pride which is artificially augmented by our knowledge of history."

This rationalistic reply to what is, perhaps, the most common myth of our time, the myth of history and tradition, is crude and ruthless in a way. But it is based on the recognition of the extreme need and urgency of this present situation, where totalitarian myths and claims threaten the whole of Europe. "We are faced with a new situation, in which a pride which is nourished from artificial sources—in other passages they are simply called myths—can be of little use. There is no proof that our knowledge of yesterday can be really useful for mastering the tasks of to-day. . . . A remembered tradition can easily induce us to believe that we have merely to carry on in order to be safe " (loc. cit., page 140).

It may be mentioned only in passing that we see here an attitude and a method of thinking which is very near to the revolutionary attitude which refuses precedents and traditions in order to master the problems which face the generation of the living. It is an attitude which doubts all myths, totalitarian myths just as much as liberal myths, Hitlerism just as much as historicism. It is a rationalistic approach carried to extreme limits.

It is, therefore, not surprising that Grisebach is also sceptical of Christian humanism, and he speaks of it as yet another myth. He discusses the " Christian æsthetes " who think they can preserve the great traditions of humanism and Christianity, of the great works of art and of thought, and that they can thus inspire their contemporaries to similar works. But the only result which he, Grisebach, is prepared to acknowledge is artistic enjoyment and a kind of European style. " But experience has taught us that through the teaching of arts no artists, no poets, no painters have been created, only dilettantes and æsthetes who have tried to avoid the problems of our time " (loc. cit., page 142). This is a hard and presumably unjust accusation and judgment, but it has sprung from an intellectual and political puritanism, which we have to acknowledge as a major force in the great struggle against totalitarian myths.

We can point to Ernst Jünger's writings in order to enlarge on this subject. For there the theories expounded in text-books and educational treatises are applied in art, and through art to what is, perhaps, the most impressive literary action against the totalitarian myth. As early as 1936 he remarks that there are signs that an elemental age is approaching. " The danger becomes more burning, and therefore pedantry, by necessity, decreases. We enter an age where one lives more naturally and, at the same time, more artificially, and at any rate under greater dangers, and Hoffmann's visions (romantic, mystical dreams) become almost real." For this frightening development he finds a kind of motto in Théophile Gautier's remark: " *La barbarie nous vaut mieux que la platitude.*" This is meant ironically, for he adds: " This is a proposition about which one could talk, particularly because it looks as if mankind intends to decide for both——" barbarism and platitudes (*Afrikanische Spiele,* page 224). As if he wanted to leave no doubt in the mind of his readers that it is the totalitarian age which he has in mind, he mentions those " huge, ugly bombs on pedestals "—the typical Nazi monument—as the symbol of this modern myth.

While there is still irony and, in a way, resignation in these remarks, there is absolute clarity in the greater work of 1939, the *Marmorklippen*. There he describes in cruel, dark scenes the horrors of the totalitarian state, the terror of the Gestapo rule, the sinister threat of Nazi myths. With a deliberate symbolism he delineates Köppels-Bleck, the " haunted place of terror ", the " cellars upon which the castles of the tyrants are built ", the haunting dreams and real terrors, the very myths of which we have spoken. He finds a rational and most human answer — " work ", " devotion to work ", " science ", " clarity of observation ", " nature " (loc. cit., page 95).

The Scholarly Approach

The picture would remain fragmentary if we did not mention those works which dealt directly with the problem of myth and mythology as their main subject. A number of serious studies of this kind have appeared, and this interest of various authors and scholars in the problem of myth, demonism and mysticism is certainly a sign of the times. Some of these studies, published in the course of the War, are serious scientific investigations which succeed in throwing light on a subject which only outwardly appears as " dark ". There is nothing of that kind of myth in classical writing, and yet there are people so very much aware of the existence of evil and the irrational that they have re-examined Goethe's writings, seeking for traces of the irrational in him (August Raabe, *Das Erlebnis des Dämon-ischen in Goethe's Denken und Schaffen*, 1942). The word " demonic " is certainly not quite adequate in this connection. But it is important to see that the author—later turning chauvinistic and even Nazi—was at work for several years on a study which throws light on Goethe's own opinions about these demonic and irrational elements. In

Goethe's early writings the existence of evil forces is expressed and pictured. Raabe points out that Goethe, as a scientist, refused to believe in the existence of non-natural or supernatural forces. You only think they are there because you have insufficient knowledge of natural causes.

But that does not end the matter. Goethe, as a moral person, finds a " strange connection " between man and evil, or rather, the demonic. Raabe explains the demonic in Goethe's sense as wild passion and despotism, which are running counter to the just order of the world (loc. cit., page 268). " Demonic is not divine because it is against reason." The human and knightly greatness of Egmont, for instance, is contrasted with " the political shrewdness of Alba, who tries to suppress the joy and independence of a happy people by war and terror " (loc. cit., page 269).

There are many examples from Goethe's writings which show how deeply that great poet was conscious of forces which man can only scantily control, and yet his highest ideal was a life and a life's work built up as rationally, and beautifully, as possible. In seeking such a life, he did not overlook those " demonic " forces which deny and frustrate the most noble efforts of the individual; they appear in many of his writings.

On a different level, Frank Thiess has approached this problem in his historical novel of Byzantium, *Das Reich der Dämonen*, published in 1941. Note again the word demon in a book title, this time chosen by a popular writer who knows what the public is interested in. The book has as its subject the history of the Byzantine Empire, and of the Byzantine Emperors and Empresses at the time of the rise of Christianity and of the decline of the Hellenic and Roman faith. In many ways it is a colourful, popular history, in many ways it is a deliberate parallel with modern totalitarianism. Totalitarianism is the demonic force we

see pictured in Byzantine history. Thiess speaks of a
" vitality driven by demons " which characterizes political
and social life in Byzantium, and contrasts it with the " deliberately self-secluded communities which have built their
inner world ", such as the followers of the Platonic and the
Aristotelean schools (loc. cit., page 430).

In a different sense these " demonic " forces appear in
Thiess' interpretation of power. " The great problem of
power is not to choose, whenever one likes, the frontiers
which one is prepared to draw, but to realize the natural
frontiers. Napoleon was wrecked because he mistook occu-
•pation for colonization " (loc. cit., page 365). It was the
greatness of Constantinople to find its " natural " frontiers,
namely, the frontiers which it was able to keep and inside
which it was capable of developing. This overstepping of
" natural " frontiers is touched upon several times in Thiess'
history as an evil development, as a demonic force.

The central part of this book is devoted to the problem of
the relationship between spiritual and demonic forces. The
spiritual forces are those of Christianity proper on the one
side and of great statesmanship devoted to the furtherance
of human welfare on the other side. Historically, he is describing the age of Justinian and Theodora. Politically, he
is dealing with the problem of statesmanship and faith.

In contrast to this real statesmanship and this genuine
faith, which is described with all possible colour and detail,
Thiess paints the picture of demagogism and myths. Even
men and masses who call themselves Christian may be
found on this dark side, carrying out wild ambitions and
sinister intrigues under the cloak of Christian purposes,
side by side with those who merely use religion as a cloak
for cynicism and graft, exploiting the masses by means of
false myths. Above all, these myths, in the hands of political demagogues, are described as the demons of the Eastern

Roman Empire. The modern counterpart in totalitarianism is clear.

A completely different field in the same realm of the mystical and of myths is covered by writings such as Edgar Hederer's *Mystik und Lyrik*, a careful study of mystical poetry, and Friedrich Georg Jünger's *Griechische Götter*, both published during the War. The younger brother of Ernst Jünger discusses the ancient myths of Apollo, Pan, and Dionysus; but he has important things to say not only about these Hellenic gods, but about our modern approach to ancient mythology in general. " Our thoughts are not mythical thoughts, but thoughts about myths. We do not think as the Greeks thought, but we think about what they thought " (loc. cit., page 6).

There, then, is a clear limitation of myths as we can see them to-day. They are ancient myths, and we can think about them. That is all. But not quite all. An important addition has to be made which is characteristic of the growing scepticism in Germany, a scepticism directed, at any rate, against the purely historical and rationalistic approach. Friedrich Georg Jünger expresses this scepticism thus: " The philosophy of history culminates in the philosopher himself, who judges the pyramid from the top. History is *Dike, Themis* and *Nemesis* for us, and lots of other things. It justifies us, and we justify it " (loc. cit., page 6). This ironical " No " to the purely historical approach is the basis for the acknowledgment that these ancient myths are, in an artistic and, for ancient Greece, religious way, something alive; something which cannot be reduced to historical processes, to ethnographical, geographical, chronological factors out of which modern scholars try to patch them up. " This is natural for the scientist and scholar; for what else could he do? But the artist, and the art lover, will defend himself against it. How could he, unless he is without any grace, place an historical process in place of that clear, definite and formed world of figures? If he does he is finished as an artist " (loc. cit., page 7).

Finally, the younger Jünger declines the interpretation of myth as symbol or allegory, as ideas or truths expressed in figures. They are something more, something which has its own life, its own beauty, its own message. Beauty and many other ideas are amongst these messages, but they are not the myth itself. For this modern interpretation Apollo, Pan, Dionysus become things or beings almost as vividly present as they were to the great artists who saw them centuries ago.

This attempt not only to analyse and describe these ancient myths, but to " see " the ancient gods, to make visually apparent their outlines and their message, may be a key to the entire problem of how and why myth, mysticism and similar things have gained such an importance at a time when the most immediate reality was the totalitarian state itself. The totalitarian state has promulgated its own myth. The totalitarian myth has been propagated and advertised with immense power and skill, and thus it has become the most important and burning issue, awakening a deep interest in the problem even where the myth itself was rejected.

The replies vary a great deal. There is the rationalistic reply, which analyses the myth and finds its real destructive and synthetic character. There is the Christian reply, which puts forward Christianity as the real faith, as against the totalitarian myth as the pseudo-faith. There is humanism, which points to the eternal values and ideals of its creed in reply to the oppressive demands of totalitarian myths. There are other strange and sometimes beautiful attempts to see eternal things, such as we have mentioned—mystical poetry or mythology, divine words or divine imaginations.

And, finally, there is the attempt to reassert the necessity
of free institutions distinct from the state, which is the
burden of the writings and teachings of Rudolf Smend,
the political scientist now Acting Rector of Göttingen University. In 1933 he was still an outright nationalist, but in
1937 we find him already standing up for democracy. It
was then that he propounded his idea that free institutions,
and the defence by the citizen of his institutions, are the
essentials of a free society. This was in a book com-
memorating the " Göttingen Seven "—those seven profes-
sors of Göttingen University who, in 1837, publicly refused
to accept the decree of the King of Hanover annulling the
Constitution, and who ever since have been celebrated as
protagonists of liberty in Germany. Smend explains that
the emphasis on the individual heroism of these men, common during the liberal epoch, was misleading, and showed
up the fundamental weakness of liberalism. What these
men did, apart from their personal integrity and courage,
was to uphold the rights of the University, of constitutional
institutions, of political ethics. Smend describes the appro-
bation which they received afterwards as tragic, because
based on a fundamental misunderstanding. " The ardent
applause of German public opinion deprived their action
of its real importance more effectively than the expulsion
by the King of Hanover." In reality these men were the
" protagonists of the *authority of the people* side by side
with the state and Government, which a people needs and
which none of the achievements from 1837 to 1933 have
succeeded in giving to the Germans ".

With still more emphasis and in more detail this idea
was developed before the Göttingen Academy of Science in
July 1943, and afterwards published under the title, *Political
Experience and Thought since the Eighteenth Century.* In
this work the various misguided attempts to find an ade-

quate approach to politics and the state in Germany are analysed. Smend holds that the romantic conception of the state was " much and rightly attacked " (loc. cit., page 521). He understands and explains the emotional approach to politics as a typical German characteristic. In this romantic and emotional approach to politics he finds the roots of German liberalism, and suggests that one of the motive-forces of this romantic distortion of politics was psychological inhibition. He quotes a violent criticism of this attitude by Hegel as a kind of madness: a " social schizophrenia " (*Schriften zur Politik und Rechtsphiloso- phie*). The reaction to this romantic trend, even in the nineteenth century, expressed itself in reactionary and authoritarian régimes. The collapse of the Parliament of 1849 is described as an emotional *trauma,* a paralysis from which the people never really recovered. Even the applause which was given to Bismarck and the newly won unity and power of the Bismarckian Reich never led " to a real politi- cal activity, to an education directed to evoke a political will and a political opinion of a really politically minded people " (loc. cit., page 527). He shows that liberalism is not strong enough to enable the individual to stand up to the new forces in the political world of to-day. The crisis is not new, but merely culminates in the course of the twentieth century and in Nazism.

The trend of thought about myth and mysticism described above is revealing. It shows a deep longing for values and things in the sphere of faith which are beyond the reach of human power and even of human judgment. It shows a deep desperation. It shows that millions of people had lost faith in everything human, in everything which might be subject to alteration or to the new valuations of to-morrow. It shows that evil things as well as good things were seen by many as forces beyond their reach, beyond their power

of control.   The fact that medieval conceptions such as
" demons " have become common property of many, even
amongst the educated classes, reveals a danger to all real
faith and belief, to all rationality, objectivity and science.
It shows that the people cannot stand the impact of totalitarianism in the long run without fortifying themselves
with a faith stronger than political argument or expediency.
It shows the longing for a faith.

But we also see that there is not one faith capable of
commanding the support of all minds and all souls.   There
are three or four creeds gathering strength side by side.
They are tolerant of each other during the time of common
danger and common spiritual antagonism.   But they are
antagonistic to each other in their contents, dogmas, methods,
Churches and groupings.   This inherent antagonism may be
overcome and, indeed, must be overcome on the basis of
a common human tolerance, without which a new period
of internal strife and hatred and spiritual warfare lies ahead.

Politically this idea is expressed in Ernst Jünger's pamphlet
The Peace, drafted in 1941, completed in 1943, and secretly
distributed.   He points to the example of Switzerland, the
United States, the Soviet Union, and the British Empire,
where " a sum of political experience has crystallized ".
" Europe may become the fatherland, but there will be many
countries and homelands."   He insists that the defeat of the
Third Reich is essential for the achievement of this great aim.
" There must be thorough justice, for there is too much blind
and senseless tyranny, too much oppression of the helpless,
too many hangmen and their stooges, too many torturers for
hell to close its doors, before they have been fully punished.
But everything depends on whether it is to be justice or revenge " (loc. cit., page 34).

IV. THE CONQUEST OF TERROR

It is characteristic of the totalitarian system that not only the idea, but also the safeguards of the individual, become irrelevant. It takes many people a long time to realize that they have been induced to live a prison life with invisible bars—but the moment of awakening remains equally frightening whether it comes earlier or later. The totalitarian state is built in a way which makes it difficult for the individual to recover from this original and deep fright. Neither will the individual find it easy to overcome his fear by action—the great conqueror of fear in war-time. In the hour of danger the soldier can always act, or at least think of action and prepare for action. The awakening individual in the realm of totalitarianism finds that it is precisely this great and noble remedy of action which is difficult, if not impossible to achieve.

This fact is so widely acknowledged by the enemies of Fascism and Nazism that up to the end of the War in Europe there has hardly been a comprehensive study or manual treating of action inside a totalitarian country. In the course of this War there have been numerous books about technical warfare, theory of warfare, political warfare and propaganda, but hardly any publications about action against the Nazi fortress inside the fortress. True, there have been numerous and brilliant actions without such a theoretical basis, but these actions of resistance and *maquis* groups have usually originated at a distance from the centres of totalitarian power. Furthermore, they have had a psychological nucleus in the national self-consciousness of oppressed nations, such as the French, the South Slavs, the Poles, and the Russians.

81

The awakening of German thought was nearer the centre of all the terroristic influences. It therefore had to be very strong and very clear if it was to survive, let alone expand. This awakening has been taking place sporadically ever since 1933, but since 1939, the year when the Second World War emerged out of the lava of Hitler's policy, it has gone on at an astonishing pace. It has led, naturally and necessarily, to the reassertion of the spirit against the overpowering threat of totalitarian terror.

"Martyrism"

This reassertion of the spirit took different forms and expressions in accordance with the group or faith to which the authors belonged. We find a deep insight into the essence and extent of this spiritual conquest of terror. "To stand up for one's convictions is a clear spiritual testimony," writes Frank Thiess, once a leading liberal novelist and journalist (*Das Reich der Dämonen*, p. 301) in 1941. "But where suffering reaches that degree of the terrifying which is literally hell, the experience of the horror releases in the individual the forces of the subconscious. Events become boundless, apocalyptic. They reach beyond the sphere of the rational." But Thiess is clear about the double meaning of this apocalyptic development. New forces of the spirit, new spiritual powers appear, but they may "turn into madness" at any moment (loc. cit., page 302).

Thiess sees this development as a danger inherent in all movements "which burn away the intellect and turn the soul of man into a volcano. If they are not carried by a generation which is extraordinary in every respect, the consequences may be unforeseeable. The penetration of the innermost regions of the soul can produce the most sublime achievements of human altruism and faith. But, if perverted, it may produce the ravings of madness " (loc. cit., page 302). Two extreme cases of meeting the terror, then—sublime altruism and faith on the one side, madness on the other side. Martyrism here, lunacy there. In between these extremes a thousand possibilities of approaching either end, or, perhaps, of avoiding it.

Thiess describes in detail the emergence of early Christianity in opposition to the absolute power of the ancient Roman and Byzantine state. There he sees both extremes and many of the intermediary stages reached. His purpose in describing these achievements and failures is not only that of an historian, but also that of an educationalist. For these early Christians did " shake their adversaries in the depth of their existence ". Their faith was so strong that some of the persecutors became themselves Christians, some of them secretly. But it was not action, but suffering, not the will to conquer, but the will to die for one's faith which proved the strongest force of early Christians (loc. cit., page 304).

It is a sociological tendency that " a mass movement of a purely passive character is in the long run unthinkable—every mass presses for action and is bound to become active and aggressive if and when it no longer feels any resistance " (loc. cit., page 306). This outlook is, however, too speculative and theoretical for a direct appeal to action against the dictatorial system, and, alas, is not meant as a call to action. It is in the nature of a hope and a promise.

Thiess himself sees the early Christians as a shining example of faithful martyrism, but the detailed history of their penetration into the state machinery of the Eastern Roman Empire is altogether more significant for their various individual actions and the growing power of the

Christian faith than for revolutionary zeal. All the same, the epic of this history provides Thiess with innumerable opportunities of describing the antagonism between faith and terror. " I do not want to teach, but to move the reader by the wealth of impressions and of tragic greatness of human efforts to win happiness," he says in the introduction to his volume of nearly seven hundred pages (loc. cit., page 9). And, indeed, the Christian approach to the modern problem of terror has become one of the most potent since 1939.

Christian Voices

There are numerous examples of Christian replies to the fearful claims of that overpowering state, and none more violent than that of Catholic Bishops and Archbishops. In the autumn of 1943 they issued a Joint Pastoral Letter dealing in fundamental terms with the " Ten Commandments as the Nations' Law of Life ". This was read in most churches of the Reich on Sunday, October 10th, and Sunday, October 17th, 1943. There the terror of the Third Reich is branded as an illegitimate, pagan, and therefore profoundly corrupt aspiration against which the Christians can rely on God's word and God's will. " God has unmasked the old heathen gods, and no people must try to raise them to their thrones again, in whatever new and refined form it may be." It is not possible to claim, as the totalitarian state has been doing ever since its emergence in the twentieth century, that it derives its power from the free will of the people, that 99 per cent —those famous 99 per cent—approve of what the state is doing, and that the state is doing it because the people want it. " No nation," the Pastoral Letter states, " must worship itself as if its will, and not the will of God, were the source of all morality and of all justice." Pius XI's famous warning is quoted: "Only superficial minds can fall into the error of speaking of a national God, of a national religion, and of making a mad attempt to imprison within the frontiers of a single people, within the pedigree of one single race, God, the creator of the world, the King and law-giver of the peoples. . . ."

The Christian claim goes further still. It reassures the masses who live in fear of their lives, who have begun to realize the extent of physical danger coming to each and all of them from the lawless fury of the ruling groups, that whatever the physical danger may be, it is a lawless power which causes it. For "the Fifth Commandment—thou shalt not kill—protects man's right to the highest natural possession: inviolability of body and life. This right is based on the rights granted by God to man. The Fifth Commandment removes the body and life of man from the reach of another man's desire to injure it. . . . No earthly power may interfere at will with the law of life and death or injure or destroy the life of an innocent man."

The Christian answer to the terror of this time is less theoretical than would appear at first sight. For it challenges the foundations of the power of the state. And even the most cynical usurpation has attempted to claim such foundations. Neither Hitler nor Mussolini had normally the courage to insist that they had obtained and maintained their power through violence, and that force was the source of their authority. The pretence of legality was only dropped in hours of desperation, when Hitler could cry that he would not shed tears over the misfortune of the German people if they ever forsook his war. Mostly and generally the pretence was deliberately kept up that even the totalitarian state was erected on the firm basis of the will of the people and legitimacy. Consequently the attack against these pretences of the totalitarian state constituted a blow against the roots of the system. At the same time it gave opponents of the system firm ground to stand on and the conviction that it was not they themselves, but their terroristic opponents, who were working the destruction of all things.

As we have seen, the Catholic approach is based on the Gospel as well as on natural law. Both the Gospel and natural law give revolutionary power to the will of the Christian. The Protestant approach is different. It knows of no natural law, but it leans entirely on the Gospel. In a somewhat primitive and really personal way, a new author writing in a military hospital in 1940, Ernst Steinbach comes to the conclusion: " The devil who tempts us is in reality our own fear of death " (*Anweisung zum Leben,* 1940, page 340). It is the most radical approach to the problem of meeting the danger of the terror surrounding us—the terror is in the last resort the threat of death. Steinbach is explicit that it is not so much the desire " to preserve life even if God demands its sacrifice "—in other words, the ordinary fear of death present in every human being—as the " life full of fear ". This " life full of fear " tries to " get through more easily by avoiding the obvious hazards and dangers of faith ".

This personal approach of an individual Protestant in 1940 is profoundly militant. " Life does not mature on its own accord. It can, in very truth, be lost if we give way to the temptation to go the wrong way and to fail in the decisive moment. The devil usually does not wear horns and does not stink. Whoever has faith does not believe in God and in the devil, but only in God."

In this strange book of a militant Protestant there is a good deal of rough and ready psychology which shows deep insight into the problems of terror and how to meet it. " Senseless suffering hurts our moral feeling, because . . .

here is no guilt, the suffering is not necessary, it comes from a malevolent arbitrariness " (loc. cit., page 284). He goes on to quote the great example of Ivan Karamazov, Dosto-evski's immortal creation: "there is no God if such things are tolerated." This is the typical human reaction to senseless suffering. But this cry, "there is no God if . . ." is not interpreted as the negation of God as it would appear, but as the expression of the deepest emotion of a human soul which does believe in God and wants to challenge God into action against these evils. "This reaction is crude and genuine." For we "have indeed the primitive conviction that we have the right to live and that nobody, not even God, has the right to encroach upon this right".

"The tragic hero" is able to go beyond this first and most human reaction. Tragic guilt and tragic suffering are recognized as possible answers to the challenge of great disasters; here "is a foreboding that the rigour of God is in reality His love, that suffering is a distinction". But this "tragic attitude" is not the real Christian approach (loc. cit., page 287). Christ does not suffer in order to achieve something, or in order to become a "tragic hero". The Son of Man suffers in order to serve, he accepts his suffering ".not as the consequence of something, not as the result of a tragic guilt, but as the real meaning of life". The lesson for Christians is that only boundless faith, without fear and without egotism, is true faith. This true faith cannot be achieved if not granted by the grace of God (loc. cit., page 288).

Again, there is much insight into the psychology of fear from which Steinbach starts in order to show the way to a Christian solution. "God can take life, but not man " (loc. cit., page 67). "Man does not make a good figure if he goes about in big boots and stamps out everything. This the rhinoceros can also do." Steinbach appeals to Matt. xiii.

28f. and Luke ix. 53-56 for support in his conclusion that "we cause pitiful, insane, incurable follies if we lose ourselves in a lust of destruction, we create results which reach far beyond our will". For those there is only one excuse— "Then said Jesus: Father, forgive them; for they know not what they do." Steinbach is very serious in this open warning to the terrorizers: "The world has been before we came; we have come later, we are not starters, but started ones. We can only continue what has been begun, but we cannot finish it. The man who tries to finish something by destruction leaves his proper sphere, he destroys the order which has created him. The result is that the law of the world turns against him, that the forces which have carried him, destroy him."

This Protestant warning ends with quotations from the Gospel: "Judge not, that ye be not judged. For with what judgment ye judge, ye shall be judged, and with what measure ye mete, it shall be measured to you" (Matt. vii. 1f.). And at last the words which sounded loudly in 1940 and 1941, as they have done ever since they have been spoken: "for all they that take the sword shall perish with the sword" (Matt. xxvi. 52).

This, then, is the direct challenge of German Protestantism to the terror and the terrorists. The knowledge that this challenge is more than theirs, that it is the challenge of the Gospe', has certainly been the source of strength which has enabled them to utter it publicly. But, of necessity, opportunities of speaking in this open and direct way remained scarce; and the strange thing is that they have appeared in print at all.

Most statements have concentrated on the fundamental questions much more than on the actual problems of the reigning terror. A typical example of this Protestant fundamentalism is offered by Karl Barth's theological writings. In them we find the deep and penetrating thoughts which have strengthened and clarified the faith of the faithful, and by doing so have helped to build up their courage, their stand against the pagan fury of the surrounding world. The firm establishment of the fundamentals, the clarification of the principles upon which the stand of the faithful should be made has become a powerful counter-point to the challenge of terror.

Karl Barth arrives at a sociological conclusion which is based on theological reasoning, a conclusion which places the Christians of our time openly and directly *vis-à-vis* the terrorists. " As a consequence of the character and task of the Christian community . . . the proper line of Christians is where . . . man is conscious of the fact that he owes nothing to himself, to his own cleverness and power, is always where there is nothing to be expected from man, and everything from God, is always where man professes humanity and humanism in contrast to a usurped pretence of godliness " (*Kirchliche Dogmatik,* ii. 2, page 804). Barth is not one of those who pretend that Christians should not care about the difficulties of this world because this world is of the devil anyway. On the contrary, " Christians are always caring for the lower, the less promising, less popular problems, even if they live in non-Christian surroundings. They stand always on the side of the minorities, always on the side of the hurt and humbled ones " (*Beleidigte und Erniedrigte*).

This is an entirely new approach to the problem of terror. The task set is that of openly taking the part of the terrorized; more than that, of siding with the persecuted. Yet it is not as revolutionaries in the political sense of the word, but as priestly companions of the persecuted. " In this disposition Christians will certainly not throw themselves against their adversaries 'as a party against another party, they will not repay evil with evil, they will not answer worldly pride with Christian pride, worldly lust of power with Christian lust of power, but they will stand up—whether the eyes of the world see it or not—for the objective good, for the common cause of humanity."

Barth's Protestant theology goes even further in the negation of violence, it arrives at a glorification of non-violence in a world which seemed submerged in a flood of terror and power (1941!) "As those who have accepted God's offer of peace they are themselves a living and irrefutable offer of peace for all men, and in particular for their adversaries. What may come of it is not within their power to decide. But as far as they are concerned they cannot be anything but this universal and absolute offer of peace. They do not fight for their own cause, therefore they cannot attempt to enforce their own right, if they are wronged . . . It is the task of the Christian community and of each individual Christian, instead of giving like for like, to give unlike for like, and to fight the ' enemy ', namely, the man who refuses to accept the offer of peace, by not recognizing him as enemy, not taking him seriously as enemy, not allowing him to behave as enemy, and thus overwhelming him. This holds true also of politics, and of the necessary political fight against anarchy " (loc. cit., page 805).

This plea for non-violence is not a plea for the toleration of terror and evil. On the contrary, it comes from the deep conviction of this great " Confessing " Christian that Christian love is the most powerful weapon in the fight against evil. But it would be wrong to deduce from this Christian non-violence that Barth and modern Protestantism following his teachings are not interested in the form of the state. By refusing to act as a political party they do not condone the totalitarian state. Barth is explicit in his denunciation of the totalitarian system, and in this way he adds to the armoury of fighting Christianity. His argument is very near to that of the Catholic Bishops of Germany, and this fact accounts for the close co-operation between the two Churches in their fight against the totalitarian system. Barth is extremely radical in his denunciation of totalitarianism in all its forms; he opposes any secular unit—be it what he calls the " social mass " or the race—being established as a " chosen community " (loc. cit., page 342). In the totalitarian state the individual is merely a member of the mass or of the people, his existence and functions are exclusively derived from the totalitarian entirety, each individual can easily be exchanged for another individual as both are merely parts of a super-machine. " The individual has to die in every respect—with his personal claim to live, with his conscience, his intelligence, his occasional opinions, and finally with his physical existence, so that the entirety, the mass, the race may be perpetuated. From this there follows that the individual has no secrets, no freedom, no responsibility, no authority, no power . . . He only lives if and when he bows and subjects himself, if and when he allows himself to be used. This conception is the exact inversion and perversion of the community founded by God " (loc. cit., page 343).

In this way Faith found a reply to the terror of the totalitarian state. It was a twofold reply, a positive one and a negative one. The positive reply was the insistence on the Gospel, on Christian love and charity, on faith. Its most solid expression has been the Confessional Church. On the Catholic side there was a different kind of positive reply, namely, the revival of natural law as affording guidance for anarchical times.

The negative reply of Protestantism as well as of Catholicism has been similar. Both have outlawed the totalitarian state as an offence against eternal and human laws and principles. In this way the Christians of Germany were provided with a clear-cut issue. They realized and publicly stated that their adversary was not legitimate, did not represent the state and the people, broke eternal laws, sinned against God. But beyond this negation Christians were in possession of positive principles and rules which they were able to hold against those under whose impact they had to live. This precious possession of a positive faith and a positive set of values and rules differentiates the Christian approach from that of the humanists and rationalists. In the individual authors or politicians, parties or groups, this difference may appear very small, sometimes even non-existent. For we have examples of powerful statements by individuals which have inspired thousands, even hundreds of thousands, of readers and listeners to take heart against the threatening terror. But there certainly has not been and hardly could be any literature comparable with the Bible properly explained and vitalized. Nor could there be an organization comparable with that of the Churches. Finally, no idea and no ideology has been able to meet the onslaught of totalitarianism with a leading group of highly trained and inspired men such as the Churches have been able to muster from the ranks of their clergy and faithful laymen.

The Humanist Answer

The humanist answer to the challenge of terror shows many single instances and brilliant examples. None more beautiful in style and language than Walter F. Otto's writings, famous already before 1933. In his essay on *Tyrtaeus und die Unsterblichkeit des Ruhmes* (Gestige Überlieferung, Das Zweite Jahrbuch, 1942) he describes one of the great prob-

lems of a militant approach to life, namely, glory. We should
have hesitated to mention this essay in this connection if
it were not for the absence of any public response to recognition of actions against a totalitarian state. The argument
that individual opposition was senseless since nobody
would hear of it or be inspired by it, became a terroristic
weapon in the hands of the dictators. The sinister silence
surrounding Gestapo prisons has become something of a
symbol.

Consequently the problem of a man's survival in the
memory of his fellow men, and perhaps even posterity, has
its importance for men who consider going their own way
in a state which allows only one road. This is what the
great humanist Otto deals with in his description of that
ancient poet Tyrtaeus, who glorified glory, the glory of
patriotism, the glory of the citizen who is killed on the
battle-field. As a scholar and humanist Otto describes the
work of the Spartan in clear and impressive lines. But he
holds against him the opinion of the greatest mind of Hellas,
namely Plato. And it is no accident that he cites Plato's
most acute criticism of the Spartan's praise of patriotism
and glory. As against the great deeds of war Plato speaks
of the great deeds inside the community (loc. cit., page 78).
" Tyrtaeus has only thought of the foreign enemy, while
there is a heavier war on in which true virtue can be proved
much more clearly, this is the interior war of parties and
revolutions." Again, even more important than this courage in internal struggles are intelligence and justice.
Courage is very necessary, indeed. It is necessary " in order
to overcome one's own weaknesses, and this victory is as
good as a victory on the battle-field ". But " without justice
courage is not such a good thing as Tyrtaeus has made out.
For we find courage in mercenaries who, as everybody
knows, are mostly crude, unjust, unrestrained and extremely

unintelligent people." Otto goes out of his way to endorse
this attack against Spartan virtues as "very convincing
to modern ethical minds " (loc. cit., page 79).

The fear of the unknown, which has haunted so many
politically minded people, is brushed aside as irrelevant.
The terror of the darkness is taken out of the daily life in
and against the dictatorial state. "Only a man who is
doing the right things is fulfilled and independent of support
or opposition from his surroundings, and even independent of
the extent of his physical power and intellectual capacities.
If he can only master himself and act justly, he cannot but
be happy, whether he be important or unimportant, strong or
weak, rich or poor."

This is the ethical answer to the terror of silence. Yet
there is another aspect, seemingly opposed to the ethical one.
It is only an apparent and not a real contradiction. For
it is' not denied that there is glory, fame, and that fame
càn be something lasting and great. "It explains the won-
derful faith in so uncertain a future and the joyous
courage which challenges a world of folly and brutality "
(loc. cit., page 94). It is the distant fame of recognition
by future generations which is meant and which is praised
as something worthy of brave deeds. This hope for future
recognition, long after death, is in some ways a typical German outlook, typical for many a great writer and musician,
and now even of political men and women.

But the more typical, and presumably also the more
powerful, tendency amongst humanists has remained their
effort to resist terror by an absolute clarity of mind and
knowledge. One striking example of this attitude is the
flood of classical studies and new translations of ancient
poetry and writing. We find a series of publications which
a new humanist publisher, Ernst Heimeran in Munich, has
printed in German and Greek and German and Latin. We

shall look at some of these efforts later. Here we mention
only some of the publications: Æschylus' *Persians*, Euripides' *Medea*, Sophocles' *Antigone*, Solon's *Poems*, Catul-
lus' *Poems*, Tibullus' *Elegies* are some of them. But we must
also mention two of the greatest translators, who have won
a fame almost comparable with that of the great romantic
translators of Shakespeare in the early nineteenth century,
namely, Rudolf Alexander Schröder and Thassilo von
Scheffer. These excursions into classical thought and
language, perhaps one may even say into perfection of style
and of beauty, have their escapist element. And who would
deny that escapism, escape into the beauty of ancient
thought and poetry, is a human form of reply to an intolerable present? But there is more to it. There is the
full realization that in this great literature of Greece, in
Greek philosophy, a genuine source of regeneration, of
thought and insight and clarity, of human greatness and
suffering, of eternal beauty has remained in being in spite
of and in contrast with the present terror.

These inherent tendencies have found expression in
writing. Sometimes they have been so clear and outspoken
that they have almost reached the explicitness of political
appeals.

" ' The great malefactors of history '—however ' extraordinary ', ' forceful ', ' astonishing ', ' colossal ', ' politically
grandiose ' and ' psychologically interesting '—remain
' profligate ', ' abject ', ' frightful ', ' terrible ' men of whom
one cannot think but with disgust." Thus Alfred von
Martin sums up what he would call Burckhardt's opinion
about the great evil-doers of ancient and modern times
(*Nietzsche und Burckhardt*, page 114f.). This analysis becomes almost sarcastic at times—when, for instance, he
speaks of the " fashionable admiration of the talented male-
factor " which, for Burckhardt, is always a sign that the

intellectual development has reached a crisis. "The un-classical want of moderation typical of an overstated individualism which thinks itself absolute and aims at 'glory through crimes' and 'self-deification', is nothing but hubris. . . . The glorification of villains however genial remains . . . in every respect a dangerous way of thinking which is in itself villainous" (loc. cit., page 115).

Exactly the same spirit is conveyed in Paul Stöcklein's *Carl Gustav Carus* (1943). This essay appeared in a remarkable series *Das Geistige Europa,* The Spiritual Europe, and in it this young historian expresses the ideal of a genuine humanism typified by Goethe's friend Carus. Stöcklein warns us against the danger of an exalted egotism, of a romantic self-adoration, so typical of totalitarian leaders. "The new force gains strength from clarity about oneself, and recognizes the necessity to serve." Man has to realize that he has his strength "not in order to follow his desires and egotism, but in order to become better and more restrained, in order to show that awe and humanity without which man remains inhuman" (loc. cit., page 11).

A more outspoken and clarifying picture is hardly thinkable. The ingenious device of ancient and modern terrorists of appearing as "great men", full of genius, and placed by their genius above all human and eternal laws, is unmasked. A villain is a villain, a crime remains a crime, however "great", however much of a "genius" its author may appear. The student of Martin's *Nietzsche und Burckhardt* is left in no doubt as to what he has to think of the terrorist, however pressing the terror may be. But neither is there any doubt as to what is demanded from the honest and decent, the real man. He sees that any thinking individual must remain receptive to real greatness. But "ethics remain always part of greatness". He interprets greatness as acting in accordance with duty " which means sacrificing one's egotism—and this is acting ethically, but by no means unpolitically " (loc. cit., page 116).

It is worth noting that the humanist approach comes very near the Christian approach here. Neither appeals for a counter-terror, neither glorifies terroristic action or terrorists as possible counters to the totalitarian terror challenging mankind. What is aimed at and asked for, is " real greatness ", " moderation ", " perseverance " and " devotion, particularly devotion which is dangerous and demands sacrifice " as against " human egotism ", " force " and " lust for power " which is " evil on earth " (loc. cit., page 117).

There is, however, an entirely different kind of writing and outlook which goes beyond the formulation of thesis and antithesis, beyond the clarification of principles. In this terror is no longer evaluated, but faced clearly, harshly. The underlying motive of this amazing approach is openly expressed by Ernst Jünger in his great vision *Auf den Marmorklippen* published late in 1939. " Only the bravest amongst us fight their way through the terror. They know that all experiences and visions exist only in our heart, and walking through the frightening imaginations they conquer " (page 94). Fear is only in our heart, and we become victorious by conquering fear in our heart.

To be sure, there is no illusion about the lack of material power of those who are facing this terror. In 1939 there was only one weapon left, " a miraculous weapon " Jünger calls it. It is the word, the word of truth, of freedom, the word of the seer and the poet, overwhelming terror by turning it into words and through these words moulding it into the horrible nothing which it really is. " We recognized in the word the miraculous weapon whose ray fells the might of tyrants." And later the deeper meaning of this apotheosis of the word is explained in the sentence: "Triune are the word, freedom, and the spirit" (loc. cit., page 74).

This, then, is the deeper meaning of the scenes of terror described in Jünger's own great writings published in the course of the War, first the *Marmorklippen,* and then his diary *Gärten und Strassen,* published in 1942. The former work is still poetical and visionary; its grandiose and colourful scenes symbolize the full terror of the totalitarian state. In the diary there is nothing but things and events personally seen and experienced.

The visionary realism, or the realistic visions of the marble cliffs correspond with the combination of cold calculation and extravagant visions in the resistance movements. The clear and cool observations of the diary of 1939 and 1940 are of immediate interest. A spade is called a spade. No doubt is left about the subject matter, namely, the terroristic actions of the Third Reich. This realistic picture of an almost photographic quality has such a dynamic power that nobody who reads it can fail to see in it a judgment. The political relevance is apparent. It is more than apparent, it is almost obtrusive if we remember that this book was written and published at the height of Nazi expansion in Europe, in the hour of Nazi victory. It is a denunciation of these victories and conquests through the medium of true description. It means that here a man, a group, turned away from the sweet fruits of victory because they saw that blood had been spilled over them; because they realized the terror inherent in its winning and in its actual possession.

The outstanding example seems to me to be the visit to the house of a village priest in Vaux-sur-Blaise on July 12th, 1940 (loc. cit., page 203ff.). The priest welcomes his unknown visitor who arrives in the uniform of a German captain. Jünger describes his humour, his friendliness, his abundant hospitality. And then he relates what the priest told him after dinner—the only conversation related in the whole book, the only story which is not his own. It is the story of how the priest and his housekeeper fled before the advancing Nazi armies. The description is short, sparing in words, as is the whole diary. But the essential lines and features appear as if somebody held a mirror up so that the victors could see how their brilliant advance looked from the roads where their Stukas were sweeping down.

" The roads were crammed with marching troops and fleeing inhabitants. Already before they reached Dommartin the terror-stricken cry went up: ' They come—les voilà!'

" Nine Stukas appeared at a great height and threw themselves down with howling sirens, shooting machine-guns, and dropping bombs. Everybody jumps from the wagons, seeks cover at the side of the road, explosions rip the road open. The priest stands up again and hears a cry: ' Throw yourself down, they are coming back.' But this was impossible for me, for I heard the cries of wounded and dying, to whom I had to give absolution. Since there were too many, I gave them the general absolution.

" At that very moment the second attack came, and the priest was thrown to the ground by a splinter which drove through his thigh. The car also caught fire so that the housekeeper was hurt by the flame.

" They carried him away on a stretcher, still hugging the sack with the church-treasure in his arm."

This is the scene on the road near Vaux-sur-Blaise which Jünger presented to the German readers in 1942. He refrains from commenting. But he goes on to describe the return of the priest to his home—only a few days before Jünger came to the village—his humour, humanity, good jokes and good food which he readily offered to a member of the armed forces which had sown death and destruction, which had spread deliberate senseless blind terror among those peaceful and lovely hills.

In these high moments when we see the visitor and the host strangers to one another, sobbing together, joking and drinking and eating and yet clarifying the fearful features of the terror threatening them both, we begin to realize the weight of this answer to the terror.

Here there is no longer any difference between the terror of the totalitarian state against its own citizens and the terror which it exerts in wars of conquest. War is branded as a catastrophe in human life (*Gärten und Strassen*, page 147). We may try to face it, or we may try to avoid it. But " we cannot avoid the issue ". It makes strange reading that on June 6th, 1940, this writer notes down these "thoughts during a ride at night " about " the machinery of death, the bombs of the dive-bombers, the flamethrowers, the various sorts of poison gas—the entire frightful arsenal of destruction which is being unfolded threateningly before mankind ". " All this is only theatre, is pure scenery which changes in various periods, and was no less say under Titus. Even among primitive tribes one is not free from these sorrows." Ernst Jünger mentions primitive man here, not as in any way more brutal than our modern states, but possibly less so. Finally he concludes that they are equally bad. " One can meet tribes who torture their prisoners in a most cruel way." This is not escapism, but an accusation: " As in ancient pictures of hell, destruction now appears always in a highly developed technical form " (loc. cit., page 148).

As the terror has remained the same, so has the answer: "the *absolute* distance from death ", eternal life " which remains eternally ". " If we are determined to go the eternal distance " between life and death, from death to life, " then everything else belongs to the imagination and the temptation ". " The pictures which we meet on this road are reflections of our weakness—they change with the times in which we have been born " (loc. cit., page 148).

Conclusion

Taken as a whole the picture which we get from this literature is not homogeneous: nor is it simple. Political, social, intellectual, and religious issues cut across each other. The readers as well as the writers are not confined to one class. We see millions of workers and peasants in the naves of the churches, behind their reading-lamps, in the lecture rooms of universities where other things than Nazi propaganda are still being taught. We find traces of them in the armed forces, in the prisoner-of-war camps in England, in Russia, in America.

The historian will not be deluded by these trends and documents into forgetting or overlooking the other side— the Nazis. On the contrary, only if they are recognized in all their fanatical fury, only if it is remembered that this is a literature and an opposition which has been created in a totalitarian state, against the impact of hostile surroundings, only then will the historian be able to read the meaning and purpose of these public pronouncements in their proper context.

Then it will become clear that there had to be a multitude of trends and expressions of free thought. Only the sum of these liberal and conservative, socialist and radical statements, of these efforts by writers and teachers, scholars and students, pastors and priests, publishers and readers created something resembling a nucleus of free thought. A short glance at what does constitute civilization even in a small country—this contradictory abundance of knowledge, effort, education, books, libraries, pictures, music, and a thousand insignificant items—suffices to give these achievements perspective. They show that the human spirit cannot be subdued even by the most ruthless dictatorship and the most glittering bribes of victories.

But this realization means little if it is not strengthened by the certain knowledge of how man, how free men and freedom-loving men have spoken and written under such adverse circumstances. It is the purpose of this essay to show at least some of the major ideas and aims which are contained in this strange literature and education. How does a free mind attempt to overcome the fear of terror which is potentially always there? How does he see freedom? What does it mean to him? These and other questions arise if we think of this problem, and in particular, if we think of the future. Is there any chance, any hope for the future? Is there anybody and anything which could be looked upon as the nucleus of a free state and society, of free thought and free education? The answer is contained in the documentary evidence, however fragmentary it still may be.

EPILOGUE

RETURNING to Weimar in April 1945, and visiting many towns in Western Germany, and finally Berlin in September of the same year, I had the strange and thrilling experience of the scientist who had discovered a formula on paper, but has yet to discover whether it works in practice. Would there be any traces of this spirit which had found expression in writings and speeches, in poems and sermons? Or would the nation appear hardened by war and defeat, petrified into a hateful Nazi block? Would there be at least a nucleus of learning and science, a small number of teachers and students of a kind worthy of the Munich students? Would there be churches filled by a faithful community, and pastors and priests inspired by the spirit which had appeared during the War? However strong the evidence on paper may seem, the moment of the final experiment, the moment when reality is met, must be a severe test of faith and scientific honesty. Would those who had stuck equally firmly to their non-belief prove correct after all?

Reality as I found it has given colour and vitality to the spiritual world revealed in these war-time writings. These authors and their audience are there. That morning in a small town on the fringe of the Ruhr valley . . . The streets were empty, it was a Sunday, and people are not up early on Sunday mornings. Suddenly a woman and a girl appeared, then more, still more, men and women, boys and girls, until the street was black with people all hurrying in the same direction. The visual impression was so strong that at first I did not hear the bells. Then I heard them, a deep and steady sound; but I still followed the crowd, expecting to be led to a somewhat sensational and quite inexplicable meeting. I arrived at a square, and there stood the church. Thousands of people going to church on Sunday morning, that was all.

Or the improvised office of the Director of Education in the Hanover Provisional Government, a house near the central park in Hanover. A long queue of young men and women, waiting in front of a door. I asked one of them, still in his uniform trousers, what he was looking for. He explained that he had just been demobilized in the concentration area in Schleswig, that he had arrived this very morning, knowing nobody, with no food and no shelter. He explained without any trace of emotion, coolly and reservedly, that he did not know where his family was because they were living in the Polish occupied parts of Silesia, and he could not go there. But he wanted to start studying, and so did the others. Later I saw the Director, Dr. Grimme. He was Prussia's last Minister of Culture before Hitler came to power in 1933, and since then a leader of the Opposition, imprisoned by the Nazis during the War, and liberated by the Allies. Grimme explained that there were many more applications for the universities than there were vacant places. Thirty thousand applications were received from prospective students for entry into the five universities in the British zone, but only 12,000 could be accommodated. In Göttingen alone more than 7,000 were interviewed or scrutinized, of whom only half could be admitted.

That there would be universities all over Germany opening their doors only a few months after the end of Hitler was more than most people expected. So there were the teachers and the students who were devoted to truth and learning and science, in spite of the many who had failed. Of course, one did not see the Nazis and was conscious of that all the time. But, then, there are these thousands who crowd the sometimes primitive, improvised rooms and gangways and lecture halls of these newly constituted universities. There are the teachers, mostly old men, often very old and haggard men, who are eager to fill the gap, or. to continue openly and with encouragement what they had to dare in face of Nazi terror for so many years. Professor Smend, whose war-time writings have contributed much to the clarification of democratic thought in Germany, is now the Rector of Göttingen University. Jaspers, Anschütz and Radbruch are teaching again at Heidelberg, and so it goes on. But, alas, there is the gap in age; the scholars and teachers in their prime of life are missing. Some there are, but not enough.

It is natural that these new leaders of thought and education should feel obliged to look carefully at their would-be students. There are too many anyhow, so that the university must select the best amongst them. So there are tens of thousands who fill in forms and questionnaires, stating their age and their qualifications, their political activities and, if any, their party membership. Members of the SS, the SD, and similar criminal Nazi organizations are banned. There is also a system of priorities for disabled soldiers, victims of Nazism, war widows or orphans. Everywhere there is the beginning of a new approach, largely dictated by the endless difficulties and shortages of present-day Germany. For who, thinking of the need for education, would have envisaged the large-scale destruction of school and university buildings? Who would have imagined cities and towns lying in ruins, as seemingly endless deserts of stone and rubble? Who would have thought of a background to education in the style of Pompeii or the Forum of Rome?

This devastation of cities and towns—Göttingen and Heidelberg are exceptions—has in itself an educational relevance the importance and meaning of which nobody has been able to measure yet. Is it a warning to youth not to think of war? Or does it harden the soul of man against scenes of destruction? This question is cropping up time and again, in the ruined streets of Berlin, amongst the red brick cascades of Kassel, of Hanover, of Dortmund. Will the child or the student, the thinking human being and the young soul in the process of shaping, accept this devastation as something final? Will they kiss the hand who is holding them down, away from work and from bread? Will they understand it as the law of the wilderness according to which revenge is justice? Altogether, how will they react to their surroundings?

It is significant for the impact of this apocalyptic existence on millions that so far no visible sign of an artistic or philosophical expression and mastery of this situation has made its appearance. No poet, no painter, no philosopher has dared to gain mastery over this misery by giving it an eternal expression in words, stone, or paint. Whatever literature there is at present is the remnant of former epochs. There are theatres and lecture halls, but it is the word of past generations which is heard there. True enough, the eternal values of true art are celebrated there now and all the time. Theatres, concert halls, or rather those miserable suburban sheds which are often used as such, are all overcrowded. Lack of interest or response? On the contrary, the managers of theatres are still dazed by the crowds which are coming night after night to classical plays. Those Berlin theatres which produced hundreds of light and entertaining plays are now devoted to Shakespeare, Lessing, and other classics. It is impossible to obtain a seat for the Opera anywhere in Germany unless one books five days ahead. In all this a deep longing for beauty is expressing itself. But there is practically no contemporary literature. Or, if there is, there is no platform, no organ for it.

My first meeting with a German newspaper not under the control of Dr. Goebbels was on the Market Square in Weimar in April 1945. The War was still on then. A crowd assembled in front of the town hall. A German policeman stood in front of it, a bunch of newspapers on his arm. He distributed them, and hundreds of people tried to catch a copy—the first news since the arrival of the Americans. Later, in September, I went into a bookshop in Herford. I asked about the newspapers, and was told that there were none. I mentioned the *Mitteilungsblatt,* or whatever the sheet was called. The man nodded—yes, there was one. It was a British paper. I had this answer from many people in many parts of Germany in many variations. They did not feel that they had yet obtained freedom of thought and expression. They felt that somebody who had drenched them with propaganda had been driven out. Somebody else had taken his place. But it was still propaganda. At any rate, they did not feel that free opinions, a free word, their thoughts and fears and hopes and ideas found expression in any of the valid organs of publicity. Open discussion, that expression of many opinions, good and bad ones, which alone may bring the necessary clarification of what is there and of what is needed, has not yet come.

There is, of course, the ever-present concern about the Nazis. He would be a bold man who maintained that there are no Nazis left in Germany, even if the leading figures have been eliminated. No, there have been too many who believed in Hitler and threw overboard all human and ethical, let alone religious considerations. They may keep silent now, but they are not likely to have changed their views simply because they have suffered defeat. It is not always the best character, judged from an ethical point of view, who gives way to defeat, and not always the worst one who is hardened in his beliefs, even if they are wrong. Consequently, one meets among the new leaders of thought and faith a good many who are concerned about those whom

they have still to convert. In those studies in Göttingen and
Berlin, in Hanover and Bielefeld, there is much thought and
energy devoted to the problem of winning the broad masses
of the people for Christianity, or for humanism, or for ethics
based on faith. There is even concern about those young
men who joined some of the Nazi organizations voluntarily,
believing in Hitler's mission. Should one leave them to
their fate? The more the individual pastor or priest or
youth leader is convinced of his own ideas, the more urgently
he insists that to make proselytes is necessary.

This feeling is almost universal amongst these men and
women. Dr. Grimme and Professor Smend, Pastor von
Bodelschwingh and Bishop Dibelius, they and all the others
are of one mind. When I took leave from Pastor von Bodelschwingh at Bethel and expressed my admiration for his
defence of the epileptics whom the SS wanted to kill during
the War, he said quietly: " Do not underline these things.
They are not important any longer. There are just as many
people dying to-day as when Hitler was still killing them.
Let us save them! "

One of the Confessional pastors in Berlin expressed this
idea in this way: " Most of the young people to-day are
no longer Nazis. Nazism was literally beaten out of them.
But they are nothing else either." A great task has to be
fulfilled now not by breaking down the Nazi bastions in the
mind and soul of youth, but by building up new bastions.
These men are fully aware of it, they are eager to do it.
But during the initial period of the post-war world their
work has been more difficult and tragic than even the most
pessimistic observer could have foreseen.

For the economic and social basis of reconstruction is
large-scale starvation, homelessness, disruption of a continued and altogether irrational kind. The fact that families were prevented from even writing to each other as late

as half a year after the cessation of hostilities, that the Red Cross with its tremendous spiritual and psychological service, with its great work of establishing communications between prisoners and their families, and between families and families, that all this at least temporarily ceased to exist in Germany, has added to the sense of frustration and devastation.

In addition there are these millions and millions of refugees, mostly elderly people, women, children, driven from their homes in Eastern Germany and in the Sudeten mountains. The endless trek of human beings has become a common sight on the roads, at the stations of Germany. Their chief and decisive fault is their race. Discrimination on political, moral, or any other ground there is none. The race is up for glorification or vilification, as the case may be. A bad background for Christian teaching, a bad example for the preaching of the equality of man. Yet it has to be done, because right is right and wrong is wrong whatever man in his madness may do. These ideas which a handful of idealists and great thinkers have propounded during the War when the task seemed hopeless, are still as valid as ever. And the many thousands of readers and students who devoted themselves to their books and sermons are not shaken by the continuance of a cruelty which they have tried to mitigate when it was perpetrated by men of their own nationality. Many talks with such people in Germany show this unbreakable faith, although it is clouded to-day by sorrow and threatened in its effectiveness by an avalanche of misery, anarchy, destruction. Starving students and hungry children need bread and butter, more than lectures. Great ideas need an atmosphere of liberty in order to flourish, not a cage, even if it is a golden cage.

There is no doubt, then, that these men whose writings and spoken words have been a shining light in the darkness of the Third Reich, are there. You can even hear an occasional word from them, and some you can meet in their modest homes or studies if you succeed in overcoming the difficulties of transport and communication. It is significant that none of these people would deny their community and solidarity with their nation, however heavy the guilt and responsibility. The declaration of the newly formed Council of the German Evangelical Church at Stuttgart in October 1945 is significant; poems of Ernst Wiechert, statements by great thinkers like Jaspers and Meinecke are in their own fields testifying to the same spirit.

" We with our people know ourselves to be not only in a great company of suffering, but also in a solidarity of guilt. With great pain do we say: through us has endless suffering been brought to many peoples and countries. What we have often borne witness to in our own congregations, that we declare in the name of the whole Church. True we have struggled for many years in the name of Jesus Christ, against the spirit which has found its terrible expression in the National Socialist régime of violence, but we accuse ourselves for not being more courageous, for not praying more faithfully, for not believing more joyously and for not loving more ardently."

Finally, Ernst Wiechert, the great poet and writer, who was imprisoned in Buchenwald, dedicates his account of the concentration camp: " To the memory of the dead, to the shame of the living, to the warning of coming generations."